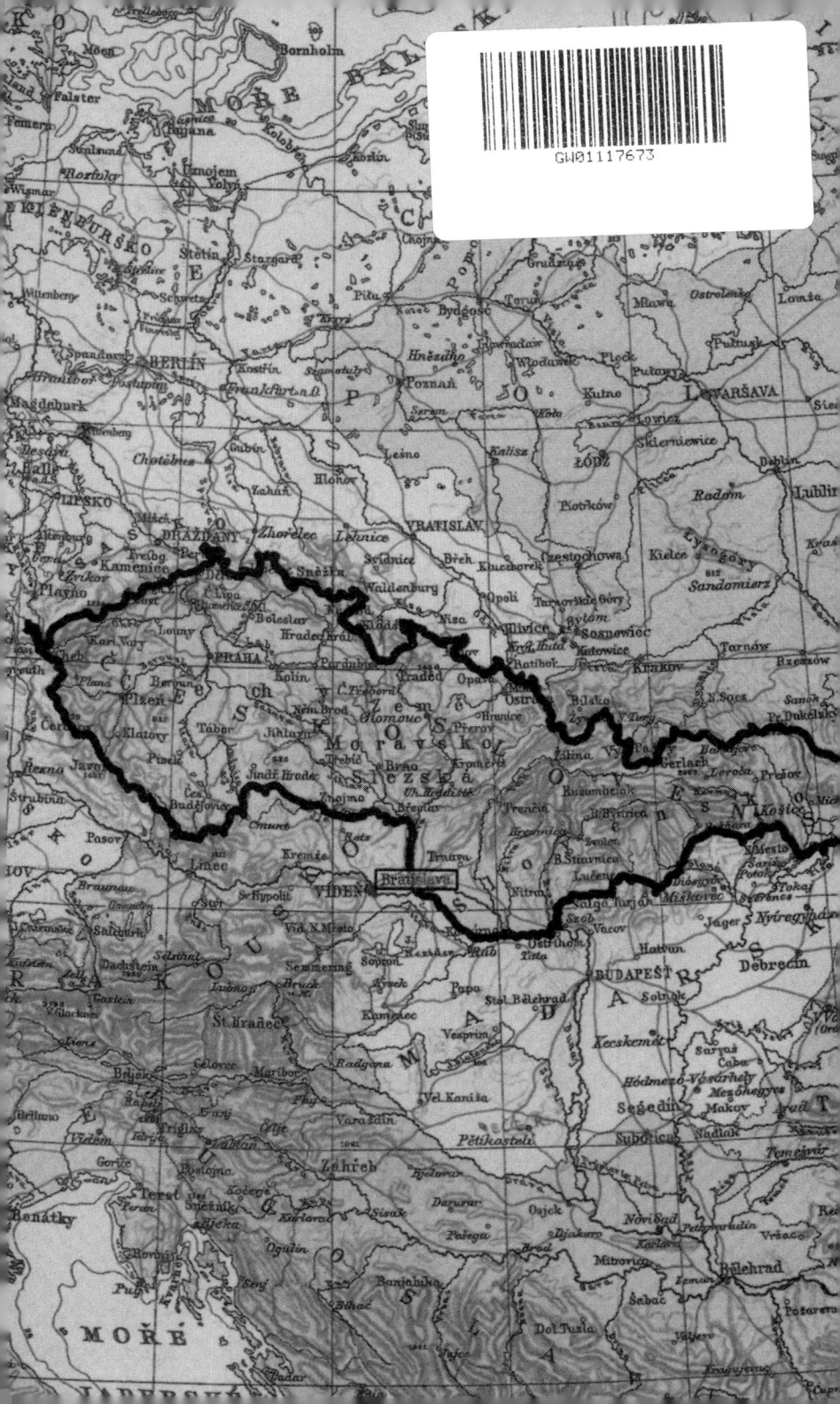

LIBRARIES UNLIMITED SOUTH WEST

Please return/renew this item by the due date.
Renew on tel. 0345 155 1001 or at
www.librariesunlimited.org.uk

SEATON 7/16
(01297) 21832

THE UNCHARTED VOYAGE

A Wartime Saga

Gitta Ogg

The Book Guild Ltd
Sussex, England

First published in Great Britain in 2001 by
The Book Guild Ltd
25 High Street,
Lewes, Sussex
BN7 2LU

Copyright © Gitta Ogg 2001

The right of Gitta Ogg to be identified as the author of this work has been asserted by her in accordance with the Copyright, Designs and Patents Act 1988.

All rights reserved. No part of this publication may be reproduced, transmitted, or stored in a retrieval system, in any form or by any means, without permission in writing from the publisher, nor be otherwise circulated in any form of binding or cover other than that in which it is published and without a similar condition being imposed on the subsequent purchaser.

Typesetting in Times by
Keyboard Services, Luton, Bedfordshire

Printed in Great Britain by
Bookcraft (Bath) Ltd, Avon

A catalogue record for this book is
available from the British Library

ISBN 1 85776 512 5

In all humility, I dedicate this book, my story, to my children, grandchildren and great-grandchildren of future generations. May they enjoy life and adventure, as I have, but may they be spared the agonies of war and persecution.

CONTENTS

Acknowledgements		ix
I	A Reluctant Start...	1
II	My Beginnings	6
III	I Have No Religion	16
IV	I Have No Mother Tongue	20
V	I Belong Nowhere Yet...	27
VI	The Childhood Diary	46
VII	Cameos From the Past	60
VIII	The Wartime Diary (The Flight)	73
Epilogue		98
Family Tree		103
Chronology		105

ACKNOWLEDGEMENTS

This is my personal story of peace and war, of upheavals, danger, adventure and survival. It covers a span of a few years and months only, a lifetime, during the turmoils before and during World War II.

The core of this book is to be found in two original childhood diaries, a faded linen-covered notebook and a bundle of scraps of yellowed paper in minute purple writing, which have survived the war.

It is the story of my 'uncharted voyage' by train, car, military truck, on foot and by sea, preconceived but completely unplanned, uncharted.

The tale runs in the shadow of the holocaust but has a nearly happy end. I have survived.

I offer these pages to my family and friends.

My special thanks to Lesley and Martin Forbes and their children, without whose help and encouragement I could not have offered this book for publication.

> Here is no final grieving, but an abiding hope, the moving waters renew the earth, it is spring.
>
> Sir Michael Tippett, *A Child of Our Time*

Route of *The Uncharted Voyage*

I

A Reluctant Start...

That is why it's important that we get all this stuff written down now, because you never know when you'll meet the Lord in the sky.

The Delaney Sisters, *Having Our Say*

Birmingham, September 1994

This is indeed Chapter 1, the starting point of the book which I am attempting to write and which so far has remained on faded bits of paper, in old exercise books and in my mind.

The beginning is in a central European township on the Danube, Bratislava (now Slovakia), during the years preceding World War II. Summers were hot and I remember days of relaxing on the water's edge, swimming, drinking thirst-quenching yoghurt with strawberry jam and sipping iced tea on picnics. I remember the first days of winter, usually around the 6 December, St Nicholas Day, when the first snowflakes would appear, school playgrounds were transformed into skating rinks and skis came down from the attic to be cleaned and waxed. I recall the smell of early spring when the snow would suddenly melt, and snowdrops, as in the French word *'perce-neige'*, would pierce the ground and there would be melting waters everywhere and very blue skies. Fridays were special days: my Father, whom I worshipped, travelled to a medical congress in Vienna every Thursday and on Fridays there would be a little surprise present awaiting me.

Life was sweet and colourful and rich and cosy, until there were rumblings from across the frontier, growing persistently. This was the advent and threat of Nazism, which even the youngest amongst us felt and partly understood. There followed family evenings where we would study the map of the world and question whether Chile or Java or Alaska or New York would offer a haven and new home. Even children understood that a new life was round the corner, both thrilling and frightening.

In the event, we finally left, a few days after the outbreak of the war, in September 1939. I can still see Bratislava castle on the hill receding; I can remember saying to myself that I would never see my home town again: but we were back that same evening. Police intercepted us and did not grant us passage. There were three more attempts before we finally got through and away.

Fifty years later I went back again. The house was still there, the façades crumbling but everything else intact. The castle has been refurbished: it isn't the same any more. But the streets in the old town felt as though I had never left. Surprisingly, strangers said to me, 'Welcome back home.'

Austin, Texas, 21 February 1995

I am picking up the pen again after a long gap. In my mind, the story has actually reached its conclusion. At moments of waiting, half-dreaming, busying myself in the kitchen, whilst listening to music or talking to friends, I have 'written' chapter after chapter after chapter, but still not on paper. Now time is beginning to run out. There are only three persons in this world who have always known me, Anny, Klári and Erica, who could confirm, extend or contradict my tale. The universal VE (Victory in Europe) celebrations in March 1995 commemorating the end of World War II over 50 years ago, the innumerable programmes about the liberation of concentration camps, my imminent 70th birthday, are all reminders of the passing of time. So far, I chose to procrastinate, in search of literary perfection and real motivation. To lose no more time, I have decided simply to do my best. The latter, the motivation, has become complex and manifold; I shall begin at the end.

My son Michael and his wife Aleta have presented me with a typewriter-printer-computer, a machine which they trust and I hope to be able to master. My daughter Lesley has started to transcribe my minutely handwritten multilingual wartime diary notes.

My youngest daughter Penny has offered to type out or arrange to type out my 'illegible' script, assuming I would not be able to master a computer, and is asking at regular intervals: 'What have you done about your diary?'

In July 1989 I visited again Bratislava, my native city, 50 years after leaving, accompanied by Michael, Lesley, Martin and three grandchildren, then again 12 months later in 1990. The second visit was highly emotional, evocative of the past and an inspiration to really start writing.

My eldest granddaughter Helen had been saying at the time of our Bratislava visit and since, 'You must write it for us, we want to know.' Jean K., a French friend younger than myself, living in the South of France, well-informed and highly intelligent, listened to part of my story over many glasses of red wine. 'Your story is European, of the New Europe. You must write for me and for all the other Europeans of my new generation.' Such rhetoric from an otherwise intimidating, taciturn person set me thinking.

After a delightful chamber music performance by a quartet, the first violinist was talking after the concert, at supper, about her life and music and family. It was my turn to answer the eternal questions: 'Where were you born?'; 'How did you come to be here?' This lovely, young, active woman simply expected me to send her very soon a copy of my completed book – she wanted to know...

Then there are many English friends who are interested,

who are intrigued and confused about my past, who would appreciate the story, who also want to know... And I have just bought a desk, neatly designed and of genuine, beautifully-grained teak, already in place at the window, in my Birmingham study bedroom. And perhaps I shall call my book *Letters from a Teak Desk* ... because I have decided to write in essay or letter form, on themes and topics as they emerge, hoping that they will link my diary into a coherent whole.

Then there is all the Holocaust literature come to light, particularly now – documentaries about the undeniably true and sordid happenings of 50 years ago.

I have escaped the Holocaust for reasons I will explain later, though the shadow was never far away. The reason why I must write my story is because mine is a tale without horror or bitterness, a tale of adventure and optimism, of an ordinary life with an almost 'happy end'.

I have recently read the books by two young women writers, *Amber Trail* and *Exit into History*, which touch on my subject: I found the two books most absorbing and close to my heart and geographically close to the lands I want to write about. Finally, they provoked me to renew my intention to write my diary: my story is perhaps after all different from that of others and I may have gained more perspective and mellowness. Natascha Scott-Stoke, in *Amber Trail*, had not lived through the war and was visiting and judging these lands with their new-found freedoms for the first time, and perhaps too quickly. Eva Hoffman, in *Exit into History* on the other hand, had a Polish background and could identify with a specific culture. I have no real roots or identity, so my case is truly different, and this is my ultimate motivation. Over half a century has now elapsed, time is running out, and I am writing this for my children and grandchildren and perhaps great-grandchildren.

I belong nowhere yet feel almost at home everywhere; I have no native tongue but have command of several languages; I have no religion but would have been persecuted for the religion and race of my ancestors. My story is not unique, but it is different, different from what I have heard or read. Above all it is the simple and true story of an individual. It is also a story of hope.

II

My Beginnings

Bratislava is a city of ancient origins which can be traced back to Roman times, and its castle has been built and rebuilt; the adjoining ruins and archaeological site of Devin-Theben on the Danube speak of the past. The Turks never penetrated as far as Bratislava, then part of the Hungarian kingdom, and at the time of the Turkish occupation of Budapest, Bratislava, then called Pozsony, became the coronation town of Hungarian kings. St Martin's Cathedral still stands in the centre of the old town. The proximity of Vienna, a mere 30 kilometres down the Danube, and the influence of Austria within the Austro-Hungarian monarchy until 1918, opened the floodgates to German and Austrian language and culture and named the city 'Pressburg'. Rural areas north and east of Bratislava at the time of the Austro-Hungarian monarchy were Slovak speaking, a Slavonic language soft and musical in sound and rich in idiom and expression. There were deep-rooted Slav traditions and folklore of song and dance and customs, recorded more accurately in the course of the nineteenth century. The political explosion came in 1918, at the end of World War I, with the formation of the Czechoslovak Republic, under the first and lifelong president, T.G. Masaryk. Czechoslovakia, a new political state in the heart of central Europe, was carved out of the large, complex Austro-Hungarian monarchy. Prague became the national capital and centre of Bohemia, now Czech lands; Brno was the regional capital of mainly Czech and German speaking Moravia. Bratislava was the capital of Slovakia and Užhorod of Podkarpatská Rus, now western Ukraine in Russia. Czechoslovakia between the years 1918 and 1939 was a modern democracy, based on western principles, with freedom of speech and equality for all minorities in matters of language, religion and rights, the state language being Czech or Slovak. At this point I should try to explain the reason or coincidence of being born and brought up in Bratislava, in the seventh year of the existence of the new state of Czechoslovakia, and the reason for my parents having chosen this town for their base and home.

My Mother (Rószi née Blumenthal) was born and brought up in Léva-Levice, a small thriving agricultural township of goose liver fame, mainly Hungarian but also Slovak speaking. It was part of the Austro-Hungarian monarchy when she was a child and remained so until 1918 when it became Czechoslovakia. After the post-Munich partition agreements of 1938 it was returned to Hungary yet again, but became Czechoslovakia once more after World War II, in 1946. Now it is in the new Slovakia.

Mother's parents, that is, my maternal grandparents, other relatives and their friends were Hungarian speaking, although purists considered their Hungarian accent and way of speaking comical and 'Slav' (*Tót*). My Father often teased Mother about her accent. The farming community in the surrounding rural areas was mostly Slovak. My Mother and family had some contact with the Slovak language because of Slovak farmers (peasants) bringing their wares to market or indeed delivering fresh eggs in beautiful wicker baskets to the house. I particularly remember Tildinéni, dressed in black with apron and head shawl, who insisted there was a little man inside this new thing, the radio.

My Mother and her elder sister (Jankus) were educated in the local Hungarian convent middle school, but only up to the age of 15, because no more education was provided for girls in provincial Hungary at that time.

The moment has come to speak of Mother's parents, my maternal grandparents, Jónás Blumenthal and Gisela née Schönstein. Jónás was the youngest of a family of five children, reared in rural Slovakia. His brothers enjoyed the good life, and by the time he reached maturity there was no money left for his education. He was apprenticed in a draper's store and studied business subjects at night, and finally bought and acquired a draper's shop of his own on the main street of Léva-Levice which he ran successfully with his wife and one assistant. Indeed it became a flourishing business known far and wide, and the Blumenthals were well-loved and respected people. I remember my delight going to the shop as a child, seeing rolls of bright fabric neatly piled high on the wooden shelves, the well-polished wooden counter, and in the centre, Opi's (Grandfather's) office like a sombre glass capsule enclosing him, his papers written in black copperplate handwriting in the light of his brass reading lamp with green shade. There was a haunting smell, a mixture of timber, fabric and mothballs. Opi was a small, rotund man with jet-black hair and a small black prickly moustache. He was always formally dressed in dark suits and stiff white shirt, with a big, fat Churchillian cigar in his mouth. How I remember the smell of his cigar! When I came home from school in Bratislava and entered the small lift to go up to our third floor, I could smell his tobacco, and I knew he was there and couldn't go up fast enough. Jónás, who had been deprived of education, became a successful self-made man and truly valued travel, education and, I think, adventure. Amongst his journeys before World War I he went to Scandinavia, and also to London at the time of the suffragettes where he saw these ladies chained to the railings of Buckingham Palace. There may have been several other journeys.

So when the two daughters Blumenthal could receive no further training or education in Léva, Jónás and Gisela decided to engage a series of German governesses to teach the girls foreign languages (German, French and English), as well as world literature and music. Grotte Jankus, my second cousin Klári's (Claire Szilard, the painter) mother, joined the trio. Photographs show the three handsome maidens in sailor dresses with their harsh, Germanic educational matrons who had severe hairstyles and ample bosoms. Governess Gretchen seemed to have had the deepest impact on my Mother.

My maternal grandmother Gisela was a most unusual woman for her time. Her mother, my great-grandmother, died when Gisela was very young and after her father's remarriage she acquired the traditional wicked stepmother. There were several siblings, most of whom lived in Léva. All of them perished together with Jónás and Gisela in Auschwitz concentration camp. They were taken there by the last railway transport in April 1944.

I know little else about my grandmother's youth but she was the most beautiful woman, unlike her brothers and sisters (my bearded great-aunts), whom Anny and I hated to kiss. She had a trim figure, always dressed in black or grey, her wavy pearl-silver hair neatly combed, with discreet glowing diamond earrings, moving swiftly and gracefully. Her first child, a boy, was stillborn; then came Jankus, Anny's mother, and my own Mother Rószi, two years Jankus' junior. Gisela must have been one of the first professional women, running the shop with her husband Jónás, as well as their impeccable and well-ordered household.

The maids, I can remember, were all Slovak country girls, trained, reared and protected by my grandmother. Mariška was their last most loyal servant. The maids remained with Gisela until their marriage and showed love and affection for the family.

The pantry shelves were full of colourful rows of preserves – something I must have inherited from her. There was festive fare like roast goose (bought live at Léva market and force-fed), suckling pig for New Year, baby lamb for Easter, goose liver for breakfast, freshly baked poppy seed bread and the daintiest variety of sweetmeats, particularly at Christmas. I remember that gigantic Christmas tree decorated by Anny and myself, ablaze with burning candles and sparklers. In the cellar covered by a slanting wooden panel door (I loved the noise and echo of running up and down), Gisela preserved strawberries, green peas and other fruit and vegetables in sand and produced these out of season delicacies to everyone's amazement, in the days well before fridge or deep freezer. There were always good smells of cooking and baking when you arrived; she cultivated subtropical greenery in the long verandah which looked out onto the garden and sheltered the rest of the bungalow, warm in winter, heated by tall green tile stoves, but so cool in the hot, dusty summers. Gisela was certainly queen of her castle, her well-oiled machine running smoothly and efficiently. She always had a little gift for everyone: a length of fabric put aside, a cake, some ribbon, a hamper of delicacies.

There were just two grandchildren, Anny and I. Because of political and personal circumstances, Anny was brought up in Léva by my grandmother and Mother (Rószi) for the first five years of her life. Therefore, she was their favourite. But my grandfather thought the world of me, mainly because I turned out to be a good pupil.

I can truly say that the happiest days of my childhood were spent in Léva, with my grandparents and Anny, my almost-sister: our mothers were real sisters and our fathers brothers.

Jankus turned out to be a rebel and left Léva at 18 years of age for the wicked capital Budapest, where she met her husband Béla Barabás, my Father's older brother, journalist and graduate in law. Erwin, my Father, was a medical student at Budapest University at that time, hard up, hard-working and not in the best of health. My grandmother invited him to Léva (in her usual hospitable and generous manner) where my parents met, and subsequently married in 1923.

Sadly my last memories of Gisela are bitter. I shall refer to events in 1939 later in my story and my last contact with her remains a very sad memory. In this 50th year after the liberation of Auschwitz extermination camp, I have been haunted by images on the TV screens of 'creatures that once were men', looking for Gisela and Jónás, looking for them... But I have failed to identify them. In the Jewish cemetery at Budapest there is a marble Auschwitz memorial and the names of Jónás and Gisela Blumenthal are engraved there, together with the other victims.

I must now turn to my paternal grandparents whom I never knew but who must have played an important role in my life. Grandfather, Bernhard Bruchsteiner and Johanna née Gutthard,

© Claire Szilard

lived in Szeged, Southern Hungary. This was Hungary's second city, on the present political borders of Rumania and the former Yugoslavia. The latitude is as southern as that of Geneva and Lyons. There were five children: Ilonka, a girl, the eldest, mother of Kitty; Béla, Anny's father; two other boys who died at 14 and in the early 20s respectively, and my Father Erwin, the youngest. Bernhard was an accountant or teacher or both – an educated cultured man. He was born in Uherský Brod, Moravia, which became Czechoslovakia after 1918. He may have been Czech speaking, although he had mastered Hungarian after settling in Szeged. He travelled to Karlsbad (Karlovy Vary), subsequently in Northern Bohemia, to take the waters. There he had a heart attack, died in 1891 and is buried there. Amongst the family treasures is his last postcard home, with a postscript: 'And how is my little Motyka?' ('butterfly' in Czech): an endearing term for my Father, a 5-year-old at the time of his death, the baby of the family.

Grandmother Janka coped with difficulty, life was hard, there was little money and many children. Both Béla and Erwin, being good scholars, gave private lessons in classics and mathematics at an early age to make some money. All five children were gifted. Béla and Erwin were sent to the top Szeged high school, a Jesuit foundation, where they received and benefited from the very best in classical education and they graduated with flying colours. There were no cars in those days, but a horse and cart was a must. Money being short, the cheapest of horses was purchased. But Neddy would pull the cart in one direction only, round and round in circles; he had been a circus horse with his previous owners.

Grandmother Janka, from photographs, seemed to be a portly woman, Victorian in appearance and dress. I know very little about her background, except that according to family legend there were a few drops of royal Hapsburg blood in her veins, of which everyone was very proud. Also she was reputed to have loved sweetmeats and was a regular at Szeged's '*Virág Cukrázda*' or 'flower cake shop'. In 1985, my daughter Lesley and granddaughter Sarah came with me on our first 'pilgrimage' to Szeged and sampled the cakes as well as the famous Szeged fish stew (*Szegedi halászlé*) but both turned out to be a disappointment.

My grandmother died a few days after I was born, in early August 1925, apparently holding Anny's photograph in her hand. (Anny and Kitty were her other grandchildren.)

Two important events must be referred to here: first of all, because of anti-Semitism in Hungary at the beginning of the twentieth century, Béla, being the senior brother, eldest child and man in the house, decided to change his and my Father's somewhat Jewish surname Bruchsteiner to Barabás, an accepted, not too unusual name in Hungary. (I shall refer to matters of religion elsewhere in this story.) So it came to be that my maiden name was to be Barabás. Second, my grandfather's place of birth, in Uherský Brod, Moravia, Czechoslovakia after 1918, determined my Father's final move to Bratislava. The situation was as follows: at the end of World War I and the defeat of the Austro-Hungarian monarchy and the victory of the western Allies, there was a series of political coups in Budapest. The first came under Béla Kuhn, a brief communist seizure of power; later in 1918 followed the victory of the 'Nylas', 'white cross', Horthy Party of fascist tendencies, and Admiral Horthy remained in power until the end of World War II. My Father returned in 1918 from the army where he belonged to a Red Cross division, on the grounds of being a medical student. During the war he was stationed mainly in parts of former Yugoslavia and was now due to resume his medical studies at Budapest University.

Erwin had always been a 'political animal' with left-wing sympathies, incredible insight and political vision. On his return he was distressed about the state of Hungary and wanted to find a way out of this political trap. He contrived an escape route, as he did indeed many more times, also in my life as this story will tell. The solution was the formation of the new Czechoslovak Republic on 28 October 1918, a potentially progressive and democratic state, under President T.G. Masaryk. Remember that Erwin's Father, Bernhard Bruchsteiner, was born in Uherský Brod, Moravia, now the new Czechoslovakia. For this reason, Erwin applied for Czechoslovak citizenship, and on the grounds of his Father's place of birth and origin, was granted the requested citizenship. He was also accepted to the German University of Prague medical faculty (Charles University), one of the oldest in Europe, to continue his medical studies. That meant readjustment and thorough studies of the German language, his previous education having been in Hungarian, a totally different language. But Erwin was a survivor, not easily beaten.

Meanwhile Léva had become Levice, Czechoslovakia. That made communication between Rószi and Erwin easier; I believe they were already engaged at that point. Erwin studied hard and gained his Medical Diploma *'summa cum laude'* in Prague in 1922. He wished to specialise in dermatology and venereology. He therefore decided to continue his advanced studies in Vienna, Austria, where he worked and studied at specialist clinics of high repute.

Later, when settled as a practising specialist in Bratislava, he still returned to Vienna dermatological congress every Thursday until the annexation of Austria to Germany (Anschluss) in March 1938.

Rószi was never far behind. She followed Erwin to Vienna in 1922 where she trained as a laboratory technician, hoping to work with her husband-to-be once he had established a practice in Bratislava. But the clientele at that period of time would have objected to the presence of a doctor's wife in the surgery.

Finally, before I appear on the scene, I would like to explain, as far as I can, the choice of Bratislava as the new home, residence and place of work.

Bratislava, though in Czechoslovakia, is situated on the river Danube, a mere 10 kilometres from the Austrian frontier and 30 kilometres from Vienna; 10 kilometres from the Hungarian border and about 50 kilometres down the Danube to Budapest, where our relatives lived. It would be accessible to Brno, and Prague, the state capital. Bratislava was Czechoslovakia's second city (and now Birmingham, my home, is Britain's second city too). Linguistically, Bratislava was a four-language town: Slovak, Czech, German and Hungarian, having attracted many Czech-speaking professional people. There was also a considerable Jewish community, mostly German or Yiddish speaking. The original ghetto has since been destroyed and was peopled mainly by trades and business people. The professional 'Jewish intelligentsia', people in the main only loosely committed to the Jewish faith or not at all, lived in the greener, more affluent parts of the city.

A true story about the inhabitants of Bratislava is that they were reputed to keep three flags in their cellars, just in case (Czechoslovak, Hungarian and Austrian), in order 'to be prepared' for change; anyway, flag-waving was part of the central European way of life!

So the geographical and linguistic scene of a quadrilingual city suited my Hungarian speaking parents, with family in nearby Levice and Budapest and professional connections in Vienna. Further reasons to commend Bratislava were that it was a lovely old city with a gem of a theatre, many bathing facilities on the Danube, a lido and indoor pools, surrounding unspoilt hills, lovely for Sunday walks or skiing and skating in the winter, a university (Komenský), and good schools at all levels in Slovak, German and Hungarian. Levice, where the grandparents lived, and Budapest, where the rest of the family resided, were not too far, an important factor for a close-knit family. So it was decided that the couple, Dr and Mrs Barabás, would rent an apartment and surgery in Štefániková 25a. The house was (and still is) a gracious old baroque building, in a leafy, wide street, close to the centre. This is where I was born on 30 July 1925 and where I spent the first five years of my life.

When we visited Bratislava five years ago, it appeared that planners had renumbered the houses and that our original home was now number 27. We moved to Konventná 17 in 1930 and this remained my real home, or 'Domov' until September 1939, the outbreak of the war. But where truly is my Home, '*Kde domov můj*' as in the first line of the Czechoslovak anthem?!

III

I Have No Religion

Austin, 23 February 1995

I have no religion...

Perhaps you can remember the reference to the changed name, Bruchsteiner to Barabás, my maiden name – Barabášová in Czech or Slovak to be exact.

I had a lovely childhood: comfort, care, love, luxuries and many friends. I was a happy child. At the age of 3 I was upset by the crescent moon; I thought the moon had broken for ever: '*Der Mond ist zerbrochen*' in my language of that moment in time. Winter of 1928 was a particularly severe one. I remember the Danube solidly frozen and I wept bitter tears because I thought the sun would never shine again (a sun lover even at that age). In the spring of that year – and there was something magical about the suddenness of central European spring with snowdrops literally breaking through the snow – my red-haired friend Liesel (she and all her family died in Auschwitz) and our 'Fräulein' or nanny were walking in the sunshine of Palacky Park, now the grounds and home of the president of Slovakia, when Liesel suddenly asked me a question: 'Gitta, are you Jewish?' I didn't know what the word meant. So she tried to come to the point philosophically. 'Do you like ham and cooked meat?' she asked me crisply.

'I certainly do,' I replied. It was close to dinner time.

'In that case,' she answered with utmost logic, 'you must be Jewish.'

The explanation was very simple. Liesel came from a strict, orthodox, kosher, affluent Jewish home. Her father, a barrister, a very religious man, often away on business, made it possible for the 'mice' (his wife and daughters) to dance whilst the cat was away. So non-Jewish fare was enjoyed during his absence.

On my return to Konventná 17, I even bypassed the customary hug and kiss but asked my parents in the doorway: 'Am I Jewish?' Both blushed to the roots of their ears and seemed to mumble. 'Am I or am I not?' was my very straight question.

They tried to explain that we were 'sort of' Jewish, but didn't really believe or practise the faith. It was arranged that I would accompany Liesel a few days later to the synagogue, my first and last visit (except for many years later on my visit to Israel when I was admiring stained-glass windows created by my artist cousin Klári.) The occasion was 'flag-carrying', a fairly jolly and colourful occasion. I can't have been too impressed because I let the matter drop.

Every night before going to sleep, I said my little verse, '*Hände unter den Kopf, ich mache meine Augen zu und schlaf' in schöner Ruh*' (Hands under my head, close my eyes and sweet dreams). Yes, German was still the language of the moment. But Jehovah or Christ didn't come into it. My parents kissed me goodnight and I didn't have a care in the world.

At the age of 6 (by then we had moved to Konventná 17), it was compulsory to start school. The establishment my parents chose for me was a Lutheran German primary school because the standards were reputed to be high and it was near home. I could have rolled out of bed into the classroom. I loved school. In Czechoslovakia, there was no state religion but theoretical freedom of worship. Nevertheless, religious education after school hours given by priests, vicars or rabbis was obligatory, or so it seemed. My slot was 'Jewish religious education', but in my Protestant primary school I learnt no Judaism at all throughout the four years. My friends and I arranged to bring lavish hampers of ham sandwiches and home-made biscuits, seated ourselves as far back as possible and carried on feasting undisturbed, allowing the rabbi to continue his solemn one-man show. Our classes were never followed by repercussions or visits to the synagogue and Judaism had no bearing at all on my happy childhood.

There were, however, events shattering the equilibrium. Sombre, lugubrious happenings in Germany: *Kristallnacht*, the burning of condemned books, and the hatred and persecution of Jews, were recurring themes in the conversation of adults. Being an only child, I did a great deal of listening. An event closer to home, in Austria, just across the border, shattered all: Chancellor Dollfuss was murdered in 1934, followed later by the '*Anschluss*', or annexation of Austria to Germany. That was the beginning of the end.

Evenings were spent in the drawing room with friends, mostly medical doctors, atlases spread out on the floor, papers, books, catalogues everywhere. My bedroom was adjoining, and of course I was eavesdropping and I always heard the questions like an eternal refrain: 'Where can we go?' 'Where will they accept Jewish doctors? Bolivia? Peru? Australia? USA?' Years later, when I saw Charlie Chaplin's film *The Great Dictator*, in which he kicks the globe-ball to see where it would land, I thought of those evenings again. In the event, we didn't go anywhere, at least not yet, but two major decisions were taken and darker clouds started to appear over my childhood.

I was to have Slovak language lessons and start at a new Slovak school in my fifth year, at the age of 10, in September 1935. German was no longer the language of culture – it had too many connections with evil, fear and persecution.

One further fundamental change was in the pipeline. My parents decided on baptism – we were to be converted to Roman Catholicism. That meant catechism classes with a priest, twice a week, as well as some learning of ritual and prayers. Judaism had left me cold, but now there was something that appealed to my emotions and senses, and I was going to make a success of it. My parents were sombre about the whole affair, and the word 'convenience' came up a lot.

On the day of days, accompanied by our respective godparents, we went through the ceremony. We were given a little cross pendant for our own necklace. I felt elated. My parents seemed gloomy and ill-tempered. I was angry with them. I was sincere about my conversion (or so I thought). They were making a convenience of it and this infuriated me. So I became a good little Catholic, for a short while. I went to Mass regularly, said my prayers and went to confession – and that was the crunch. The priest confessor knew instantly that I was a new convert and he humiliated me totally. I felt forsaken. That was the end of my Roman Catholicism.

My parents and their family before them were of Jewish race, of Jewish blood, but not of Jewish religion. My maternal grandmother, Omi, was perhaps a case apart. Although she only worshipped at home, she fasted (Jewish style) and feasted in the Christian manner at Christmas and Easter-time: '*hátha*' in Hungarian, meaning 'just in case'.

Hitler's anti-Semitism was racial cleansing towards the ultimate solution: the eradication of all Jews. Thus we, like so many others, had to flee, had to go on the *uncharted voyage* because of our heritage.

In my early teens, first France, then England, became my havens, my lands of peace, where I felt free to be myself, free to believe or not believe. May this continue for ever. My heartfelt faith is perhaps the eternal ideal of religious and political freedom, equal rights and humanity.

IV

I Have No Mother Tongue

I have no mother tongue but many tongues. Both my parents were Hungarian speaking, and that is how they spoke together. The Hungarian language is rather special, different from most other European languages. In Hungarian there are vast regional differences in accent and emphasis. Mother was from Léva and her Hungarian was almost Slovak sounding, crisp and laconic. Father came from warm, southern, colourful Szeged, with poetry and song for every occasion in his daily speech. My parents had a deep belief in culture, in the best sense of the word. They were well educated, well read and had open minds. They felt sincerely but perhaps not correctly that Hungarian was not a language of culture. After the collapse of the Austro-Hungarian monarchy the new 'Renaissance' of post-war 1918 Europe, according to my father's thinking, was in the language of Goethe, Schiller, Heine and Mann. They felt that German could be a European language within post-war (1918) Europe. They both had a fair command of German. So it was decided that German was to be my language, 'my tongue'. They would speak, read and sing to me in German and I would be sent to German schools.

The German era

It is important here to comment on the constitution of the Czechoslovak Republic which insisted on linguistic and religious freedom for all citizens, as well as the provision of schools to serve all linguistic minorities.

So German was my starting point. At the age of 5, I wrote a booklet, in German of course, which my mother bound in silver paper, and the subject matter was weather (*das Wetter*). I went to German kindergarten and had four years of German primary schools. I spoke in German with all my little friends, relations and adults. The books I read were German, or translations of classics into German; so were the songs and rhymes. I wrote my first diary in German. Differences of accent always intrigued me and I would listen hard to the market people in Bratislava and repeat what I heard. 'Pressburger German' has sounds close to the Viennese accent.

But there were changes in the air, political and personal. The implications of 1933 and the advent of Nazism in Germany with further repercussions were felt strongly. The burning of books – *Kristallnacht* – was a death knell for German civilisation and clouds were darkening, or so I gathered. Thus it was decided that German was no longer a language to be proud of – and in any case we lived in Czechoslovakia, Slovakia to be exact.

The Slovak era

I was to have private lessons in Slovak and change schools in my 5th year, in 1935, at the age of 10. Learning Slovak was no great problem, and after a year of Slovak primary school I graduated to Slovak grammar school where I remained until we left in September 1939. So my education was now to continue in Slovak, and slowly but surely writing, reading, school work and talking became Slovak, except for communicating with my parents in German. I loved the new sounds and the logic of Slovak grammar as summarised in textbooks – (*pravidlá jazyka slovenského*) – all of the rules and exceptions of the Slovak language, in one complete book. My reports were good and I always enjoyed school as well as the new challenge.

French

Meanwhile, in addition to piano lessons, I also had private French lessons from the age of 10. My teacher was a Madame Kumayer whom I shall never forget. She was big, grey, wonderfully dressed in pastels with lots of jewellery and dangly earrings. She only spoke in French to me – no foreign word would cross her lips. Early in the course of tuition she introduced me to subjunctives and other grammatical complexities and she also insisted I learn a poem about Mary Stuart leaving France before her decapitation and death: 'Adieu mon pays bien aimé'. Did she identify herself with Mary Stuart, having left her beloved France (Alsace to be exact) for ever? It was also rumoured that she was married to a German Nazi. When later I read Corneille's *Horace*, where opposite warring sides are linked through marriage, I did think again about Madame Kumayer and her love life.

She must have taught me well because I found French lessons at school much too easy. I remember mass-producing French examination answers under the desk, for my fellow pupils without being discovered.

The Slavonic heritage

I referred earlier to the presence of many Czech professional people, teachers and others, within Slovakia. As there is a wealth of Czech literary treasures it was assumed in my Slovak school that all pupils would automatically have a passive and active command of Czech. There are some differences of grammar and vocabulary and considerable differences in pronunciation between Czech and Slovak (though nothing insurmountable) and a Slovak can understand a Czech and vice versa. We had several Czech teachers who were competent and popular.

After the Congress of Munich in 1938 and the subsequent political changes of 1939, such as the occupation of Prague, Bohemia and Moravia, Slovakia became an independent decimated state without political glory. The exodus had started, the floodgates opened and there were waves of emigrants, mostly Czechs leaving Slovakia, also some Jews finding a promised land somewhere else. Some Slovaks were resettled within Slovakia. The consequence in terms of schooling was the departure of beloved teachers, upheavals and general confusion. Politics and our lives were intermingled and my diary entries, as will be seen later (mostly in German with some Slovak), deal with politics and personal upsets, all in one breath. I remember being very well informed and politically orientated. On the way to school on the tram, I managed to read grown-ups' newspapers upside down in German, Slovak or Hungarian.

I also learnt to play truant because I lost interest in school and the atmosphere had become unpleasant. My report (the last one) showed 92 hours' absence: I typed my own excuses and forged my Mother's signature when she was not prepared to confirm my absence. By then my Father had already left for France.

Whilst at home instead of school, I raided the bookcase and read everything I could lay my hands on, without truly understanding. My study of Father's multicolour illustrated medical textbooks on venereal diseases worried me greatly – I imagined I was smitten by every conceivable ill.

But now back to school: we had a geography teacher called Otilka Vonášková, Otilka to us, a native of Yugoslavia. She had a funny accent, she was tall, spindly, with a highly coloured face and lots of pimples and a grey bun. I found her very comical. One day she gave us a lecture which at that moment in time had no meaning and we giggled. 'Detičky' (little children) – and we were 13 years old – she said, 'be proud to be Slav! We are all brother Slavs, Slovaks, Czechs, Poles, Yugoslavs, Russians! We can understand one another! We are brothers and sisters.' Her words have come back to me time and again, and Slovak has proved to be a Slavonic passport.

I am now in France, October 1939, in a new environment, a new school, speaking French, nothing but French. Madame

Kumayer must have helped. Next to me sat a girl called Olga Scherer; she was a 'refugee' or 'foreigner' like me, but she was Polish. I discovered that I could speak to her in Slovak, that she would reply in Polish and we would understand each other perfectly.

Much later again, in 1947, when I was living and working in Blackburn, England, I sought Russian tuition. Chance would have it that my tutor was called Chad Varah, the founder of the Samaritans. He presented Russian so clearly, the structure and vocabulary seemed so easy and so much like Slovak that I understood most of it. But we had so much else to talk about, things more vital than language study, and I never got very far with Russian.

In the post-war years I loved my travels and holidays in peaceful former Yugoslavia. I could adapt my Slovak to Serb, Croatian, Bosnian and Albanian, and make myself understood; and when all failed I put on a foreign-sounding German accent (Yugoslavs had bitter memories of Germany) and got by that way. Otilka was right again. On my return to Bratislava in 1991, 50 years later, having spoken no Slovak at all for half a century, I was lost at first. But with wine and food and goodwill, words came flooding back once more.

French again

France, French school and the French language were a delight for me: the sounds, the feel, the music, purity and fun. I thrived on it. At first my marks at school were mediocre, but soon improved. In Paris, a few months later, I made friends with Jacqueline Eydelmanth, and she helped me discover Paris during the 'peaceful war' before the fateful June of 1940. She was a Parisian, French speaking, but her divorced parents were Slavs: mother Polish, father Russian, and I could speak with them. Jacqueline from Pigalle, 11 rue Labruyère, remained a lifelong friend.

Hungarian

But how was I to converse with my parents in Paris, in 1939, in a country at war with Germany? German in wartime Paris was hardly the language of communication and certainly not to be overheard by others. My parents' command of Slovak was inadequate. My Father, always a cynic and full of bright ideas, said that the French (*szürke*, grey in colourful Hungarian) would not be able to tell the difference between Hungarian and Czechoslovak (a language which does not exist at all). He suggested that we talk Hungarian and pretend it was Czechoslovak.

And that is precisely what happened. I must have acquired a command of Hungarian passively whilst listening because I was never taught and had not spoken it in the preceding 14 years. But from that moment on (we were standing on the corner of Boulevard Magenta and Rue des Petits Hôtels in Paris), my parents and I only spoke Hungarian together until their death. I somehow managed to learn to read and write Hungarian as well.

English

In my Parisian grammar school, Lycée Victor Hugo, we started English lessons which I enjoyed. The textbook had a pale blue cover and was called *L'Anglais Vivant*. Lessons were short-lived because we had to leave Paris six months later in June 1940. I don't know how much I had learnt. In my diary several months later, on the boat HMS *Reina del Pacificio* on the way to England, I wrote that I had a dream in English, before landing at Liverpool on 28 October 1940. Polite English ladies in an elegant drawing room were delicately sipping tea out of decorated bone china cups, eating toast and marmalade, chatting together. I can't really remember ever learning English.

Then followed my education in English schools in London and Canterbury. I remember the euphoria of feeling safe, after our travels through Europe. There was help and goodwill everywhere. My school, Southgate County School, Palmers Green, London, was a new world. It was wartime Britain, total blackout, food rationing and bombs, school canteen lunches and sago puddings. To me, then aged 16, it was like paradise. Mr Squire, the English master, gave me extra lessons; Miss Burns, the maths teacher, helped me regularly. My Father, the eternal student, drilled me in the command of English, often against my will. I loved the deductive logic in the study of geography and history, using maps and documents, after futile methods of rote learning in Bratislava and Paris. English took over in every way. One year after arriving in England, I took the matriculation examination, gained very good results and a distinction in English language. The essay subject I chose was 'Frontiers' – at the age of 16, I was quite a specialist in that field. I must have crossed many more frontiers than my English-born contemporaries. I can honestly say that English has become my principal language after more than half a century in Britain.

But I love to return to the Continent for longer periods and be immersed in Hungarian, French or Slovak. Ironically, but not surprisingly, I became a teacher of modern foreign languages and taught for many years in a Catholic secondary school.

I still have deep misgivings about the German language, although I still count and sing nursery songs to my grandchildren in German. Is it perhaps my mother tongue after all?

V

I Belong Nowhere Yet...

Czechoslovakia

When I was little, my family was everything: Mother, Father, my very loving parents; my grandparents in Léva-Levice and my much loved cousin Anny. That was my world.

Now and again at holiday time, we took the train, because we had no car. Departure meant excitement and anxiety, leaving that cocooned security. We went outside that world, required tickets and permits and papers and passports and visas: this was central Europe, even before 1939. At stations and frontiers were hoards of ominous looking men in uniform, porters in striped linen jackets and red caps milling around and probably losing our luggage. No one knew which platform for departure of the train, nor did anyone know the times. My Mother was always very excited and worried and passed this feeling on to me. Father would get off the train at stations where the train stopped to buy papers or drinks and get on again at the very last moment, and I feared that he would miss the train and have to stay behind. Fear for my Father was a recurring childhood nightmare. But I 'belonged' to my parents and they to me.

The concept of nationhood crept in later, more precisely after I had started at Slovak grammar school in 1936, when the foundations of central Europe began to shake. I began to be aware of this land Czechoslovakia where I lived and which was my home. Civic teaching must have been thorough because we studied the constitution (*Ústava Republiky Československej*), learnt all about historic moments of glory and defeat (I still know the dates), about national legend and heroes. We learned about the founders of the Republic, in particular about Tomas Garigue Masaryk, the first president.

I still have my original *School Atlas of Geography* where there are many pages of maps about all aspects of the geography of Czechoslovakia, but only a few pages about the rest of the world. The atlas *History of the World* showed the same emphasis, and the history of the rest of the world was again conspicuous by its insignificance or even absence.

I soon learnt that grand sentences glorifying the greatness of this land of ours, Czechoslovakia, would earn me extra marks in my Slovak school essays. Tongue in cheek, at the age of 11, I indulged in this patriotic style of writing.

Semblance and premonitions became reality. First there was the general mobilisation in October 1938 when my Father, together with thousands of others, was called up to be a soldier for one whole week. Our country was in danger! We must defend it! The apparent danger passed momentarily but things never returned to normal again.

I remember the Conference of Munich in 1938 as though it were yesterday. I felt deeply like the rest of the nation; yes, suddenly I had discovered nationhood and love for my country. I felt, like all grown-ups, that the West (Great Britain and France) had let us down, had forsaken us, that the grand carve-up of Czechoslovakia was about to take place because the rest of the 'free world' didn't care for a little sausage-shaped land, the little Republic 'whose name was unpronounceable' according to British Premier Neville Chamberlain. It was supposed to have been a sacrificial offering for the sake of world peace. I can still see in my mind's eye people in the street weeping unashamedly. I also wept. They had forsaken us and we were destroyed.

Yet our little Republic had been a model state since 1918, based on British, French and American ideals and principles of liberty and government. We had political, religious and linguistic freedom, free education and a progressive health service. Didn't they understand? We had mottoes like 'protect the child' and the state motto 'truth prevails' (*Pravda vítezí*). Now we were in a shambles: it was the beginning of the end. At 14 years of age I mourned for my home and Fatherland, my Czechoslovakia, in all my sincerity.

Extracts from my childhood diary written in German throw light on this world, where politics, danger, school and family life and general chaos become intermingled. We left Bratislava on 12 September 1939, days after the outbreak of World War II. Our departure was fraught with danger because Slovakia, no longer Czechoslovakia to all intents and purposes, was already occupied by Germany, although German uniforms remained as yet inconspicuous.

The journey was illegal, we had no right or permission to leave, a taxi was to take us across the border to Hegyeshalom in Hungary (at a considerable cost) and we were to travel further from there by train to Budapest. I tried to remember forever Bratislava Castle on the hill, the view from my bedroom window at home, the river Danube and the spires of the old city, as the taxi sped along the dusty road towards the frontier. I felt I would never see them again. But the guards stopped us in our tracks. We were not allowed to cross the frontier, and returned ingloriously back home, that same evening, along the same road, and to a totally empty house. What an anticlimax! We resumed our journey to cross the border into Hungary one day later on 13 September 1939, and this time we succeeded. Before finally leaving Slovakia we were searched and I remember feeling so humiliated because of the thorough frisking and personal probing by the women frontier guards.

We arrived in Budapest where we stayed several weeks with our relatives. It all seemed endless and I can remember little about it other than the feeling of deep impatience to get away, to France, to my Father. During those weeks of procrastination, transit visas through Yugoslavia and Italy, our planned route, expired and had to be renewed at the different embassies, at more cost; residence permits in Hungary had to be extended accordingly, and it was an endless trek to offices and embassies. Meanwhile I was sent to the nearby Budapest convent school for French lessons. I can just about remember the first line of the Lord's Prayer in French: '*Notre père qui est aux cieux*' being drummed into me by an austere-looking nun. My Mother went to dressmaking classes, the eternal preoccupation with training in order to find a livelihood in our 'promised land'. Finally, the great day came and we left for France, through Hungary, Yugoslavia and Italy towards Modane, the Italo-French frontier. The railway carriage was very crowded and there were many Italian soldiers in their khaki uniforms and Tyrolean-type hats with bushy feathers. Italy was not yet at war, not until 1940, but military manoeuvres were apparent. At that moment I was not at all troubled by politics. We were on the move, due to meet my Father shortly. The train was chugging through gigantic snow-covered mountains, whizzing through tunnels, and the soldiers in the compartment were singing loudly and melodiously. It reminded me of the chorus of *Il Trovatore* and other Italian operas.

France

We were approaching the French frontier at Modane. At last, without problems and so easily, we crossed the frontier, and we were on French soil. I imagined that the air smelled different, that the soil was pure and that we were in fact in paradise and safe and without fear. Soon we were to reach Vichy, where my Father was waiting anxiously at the station. It was 28 October 1939.

I adopted France and France adopted me. We were together again: Father, Mother and I. Home was being together wherever.

France was already at war, but until June 1940 there was no action, no fighting. One almost forgot that the war was on.

We lived until the end of December in Vichy where I went to the local school, École Primaire Supérieure. We rented a room in a boarding house, Villa Magali, rue Mounin, and took our meals with the other residents, mostly retired long-faced people who seemed ancient to me. We weren't affluent but I can't recall any deprivations. Vichy, a spa town, seemed gracious and calm, with many large trees and imposing hotels. People were still 'taking the waters'. I enjoyed my contact with the French, those of my generation and older people, although there were several central-European refugees in my parents' circle. I loved my new French school; I felt very happy, free and at ease.

For reasons which are not totally clear to me, we only stayed two months in Vichy, and in January 1940 moved on to Paris. Perhaps the reasons were financial: Madame Doulcet, a friend, put her apartment in 7 Rue des Petits Hôtels, between the Gare du Nord and the Gare de l'Est Paris, at our disposal, for very little rent or perhaps free of charge whilst she and her family decided to move away to the country in order to live in their house at Espalion, Aveyron, near Rodez. Several French families had foreseen danger in the city and decided to evacuate to rural areas where the war was less likely to affect them.

Our new home, the apartment on the 4th floor, was minute compared with Bratislava, but it was comfortable and lacked in nothing. The kitchen could have been part of a dolls' house, and the wide range of culinary gadgets mesmerised me. The bathroom had a washbasin and bidet, but no bath. I had my own room once more and felt very comfortable.

The market hall, Marché St Quentin, was almost next door, on the corner of Rue des Petits Hôtels. In those early war months France was still a land of plenty and I remember my delight going from stall to stall, admiring mountains of colourful fruit and vegetables, some of them new to me, and varieties of so many cheeses. You could buy ready-cooked beetroot and ready-peeled new potatoes kept white and fresh in buckets of ice-cold water. I remember the wonderful taste of the first globe artichoke dipped in oil and vinegar dressing. In the humblest café it was red or white wine without question, and always bread on the house. I had to wait many years before becoming acquainted with the glories of French

PARIS MARAIS

© Claire Szilard

gastronomy: my Father had suffered from duodenal ulcers ever since I can remember, and my Mother's cooking followed a rigorous and dull diet for the three of us, except for her excellent gateaux.

Paris was dressed for war, although it still didn't seem real. There were sandbags enveloping and protecting statues, monuments and façades. There was a not very strictly observed blackout in the whole city. In the sky you could see Zeppelin-like silvery-grey balloons, supposedly protection against air attacks. Gas masks were to be carried by civilians and there was provision for air-raid shelters, but for all this Paris remained a city of wonder, beauty and peace and I fell in love with it. I knew my way around the city by bus, underground and on foot. For 90 centimes you could remain underground all day and I knew all the stations by heart. I felt free, safe and exhilarated.

French schooling was a revelation. Lycée Victor Hugo, Rue

Sévignée, in the Marais district, was to be my new school. The building goes back to the seventeenth century and is in keeping and character with the other splendid buildings, 'hôtels', of the area. I passed Place des Vosges, the most beautiful Parisian square, on my way to school.

At the Lycée, French literature impressed me for ever. Madame Finaton was the devoted, fanatical and formidable teacher and she expected, and got, very high standards. 'Lecture expliquée', the study of literature through texts, with structural analysis, appealed to me very much and I learned to love and appreciate the French classics. Also, in spite of war, I was taken to the theatre now and again, and saw plays at the Comédie Française, as well as operas and operettas in Parisian theatres.

The ancient Lycée building did not exactly lend itself to scientific subjects. I remember struggling with geology without ever having seen or touched a pebble. Learning by rote did not mean a great deal, nor did it reveal geology. Physical education proved to be somewhat restrictive as well. I don't think there was a gymnasium. Physical exercise consisted of gas mask drill: putting them on and taking them off again, usually in the ornate courtyard.

As for needlework, never my forte, politics came into it yet again: spring 1940 coincided with the USSR invading Finland and briefly, to the world's surprise and astonishment, joining forces with Germany. So it was ordained that all 'Lycéennes', pupils of Victor Hugo, would make checked gingham overall aprons for Finnish girls. I don't think I ever finished mine because Hitler was to invade Paris that June, 1940.

I had several good school friends, Jacqueline Eydelnanth in particular. Life was good and full. I really liked living in Paris and could have stayed there for ever. By now I talked, thought and dreamed in French. But for subsequent events, I might still be there now; I would most certainly have become a French citizen.

The agonising months in Bratislava leading up to the outbreak of war and our departure, only six months before, were far away, the agonies almost forgotten. My new home and country, France, however, was to have a similar fate in store, and all too soon! By May 1940, Germany had invaded Holland, Belgium and northern France, and German battalions were heading towards Paris. We could hear the rumbling of machine-guns and war noises in the distance. Soon, more and more vans, lorries and horse-drawn carriages, laden with human beings, bags, bedding, birdcages and tatters were rolling down the boulevards, including Boulevard Magenta at the end of our road. Paradise was going to be short-lived. The country I had come to love, where I seemed to be accepted, was to capitulate. The words of the French President Paul Reynaud, declaring Paris *Ville Ouverte*, 'Open City', to save the town from destruction, still ring in my ears. It was the beginning of the end yet again. I mourned for France as I had mourned for my first home, Czechoslovakia. France still remains one of those very special places for me, perhaps my second home!

Great Britain

It is now the end of October 1940, and the scene is England. We arrived here completely by chance, after five months of unplanned, uncharted travel. I shall write later in detail about this period based on my scrappy daily diary notes. Let me describe now the country where we landed on 28 October, and where I have chosen to live ever since, my permanent home and base.

We landed in Liverpool and disembarked from our boat, HMS *Reina del Pacifico* after some form of quarantine. A bus took us to a railway station, I presume Lime Street, where we were to get on a train, destination unknown. It was a night of nights, moonless and black; the train stopped frequently, the stops were preceded and followed by noisy explosions and 'fireworks', hell let loose. Miraculously, the train and passengers arrived unscathed, in the early hours of the morning, in London. This was the London Blitz, air battle, at its fiercest. My parents and I, and those other fellow travellers with whom we had shared Mar Azul, Caxias Prison, HMS *Neuralia*,

Gibraltar and the long voyage on HMS *Reina del Pacifico* were all together. We were taken to a reception centre at North Norwood, South London, referred to as 'purgatory' by our cynical fellow travellers. We were fed, clothed, kept warm and together. Gradually, important looking people started to come, singling out individuals or family groups; we must have seemed a strange motley bunch of travellers, and we had to be vetted and examined; spies might have been amongst us; some of us could have been a danger to a country, Great Britain, very much at war.

One day, representatives of the Czechoslovak government in exile, London, came to Norwood and talked to my parents at length. We passed 'the test', were found to be genuine and were released. Immediately we were issued ration books, provisional identity cards and an address in the East End of London, our new home! We were launched for our new life in England, at 15 Ickburgh Road, Hackney, London, E5. The house was in a row of houses, brick-built, with front and back gardens, close together, all houses identical, such as I had never seen before. The only noticeable difference was the extent of war damage, wreckage or desolation. We were to share this house with a Belgian couple who had escaped from German-occupied Belgium. The only furniture or furnishings were mattresses, a table, chairs, two saucepans and blackout material. In the downstairs room there was an open hearth or fireplace, and trees and wood in the garden. Because there were no tools to be found, the men dragged whole trees from outside and pushed them into the hearth already alight with newspaper. The trees were burning away into smaller more manageable logs. Soon kind-looking ladies in uniform called, asked some questions and left blankets and some warm clothing and made practical arrangements for money and so on. The rent was paid for and amounted to 30 shillings (£1.50) per week. Mother received a weekly sum of money, I think from the labour exchange, which seemed to be sufficient for food from the local shops. The air-raid sirens went often during the day and there were regular nightly air-raids. At first we went every night, before darkness, to Hackney Park

Anderson air-raid shelters, and took blankets, drink and books with us. Henry Moore's picture, *The Air-raid Shelter*, depicts the scene as I remember it. The other families in the shelter were kind, jolly and warm-hearted. By now we were well into November; it was damp, cold and bleak. My Father, still the decision maker, decided that statistically the danger of pneumonia contracted in the damp air-raid shelter was greater than a direct hit onto our downstairs mattress in Ickburgh Road. So henceforth, we watched the glowing branches in the hearth growing smaller, listened to the planes overhead, learned to recognise friend or foe up above, heard the whistle of bombs falling nearby and slept in our cosy, intimate home.

I really can't remember being afraid, neither in Ickburgh Road, nor later during numerous air-raids. Having survived so many dangers, death and the fear of horrors and persecution, perhaps I felt immune or ever hopeful. At worst, it would have been a clean death, amongst family and friends. But above all, I wanted to live, in my new found home and country, discover the new life, grow up, live and be free.

Our conditions in Ickburgh Road must have been grim, or so I was told by Erica Konstantinowsky, my friend from Bratislava. I was certainly not distressed: I was with Mother and Father, neither cold nor hungry, I was not pursued by the German armies.

Christmas 1940 was approaching. My parents had with them an address book and wrote a few Christmas cards to old friends already settled in England who had come directly, straight from Bratislava, to tell them we had arrived. One such card brought a dramatic response and changed the shape of things to come: I mean family Konstantinowsky from Bratislava.

The minute our Christmas card had reached them, Kurt, Ida and Erica set out to Ickburgh Road. They were shocked and horrified by what they saw and the conditions in which they found us. That very same afternoon I was to pack a small bag with basic needs and possessions, say goodbye to my parents, and follow them to their home in North London, Palmers Green. The Konstantinowskys had left Bratislava and came directly to London where Kurt, a great physicist, was offered a situation. They had brought with them most of their belongings and the flat in Green Lanes was furnished very much in the style of 'bourgeois' Bratislava. A move is naturally accompanied by upheavals, but in their case it was simpler and they had not suffered the trauma of those who left later, or had to escape from France as we did. The Konstantinowskys' life in London was, therefore, almost as well-regulated and comfortable as I remember it to have been back home in Bratislava.

Kurt and Ida could not do enough for me, then 15 years old, just one year younger than their own daughter Erica. I was given a bedroom with crisp sheets; the meals were copious and well prepared. Ida got out the sewing machine and altered and made new clothes for me. I was to find a room or rooms in Palmers Green for myself and my parents, safer and calmer than Ickburgh Road, Hackney, less harassed by air-raids and desolation. The sum allowed by National Assistance for accommodation was still 30 shillings a week.

With the Konstantinowskys' help we found an advertisement in a shop window in the high street and followed it up: 142 Hedge Lane, with Dave and Shirley Rabbie and, 10 minutes' walk from the Konstantinowskys. The Rabbies were a Jewish couple, Dave a taxi driver, and they had a little daughter Carole, a dainty curly-head resembling Shirley Temple from the films I had seen. They gave me a lovely welcome, accepted my family and myself even before they had met my parents, and were satisfied with the 30 shillings rental. We were offered one larger and one box room, slightly furnished, on the first floor of their 'upstairs-downstairs typical house', with bathroom and toilet to share. We stayed there nearly 18 months, until my Father started to work as a doctor of medicine again. I remained in touch with the Rabbies, our very dear friends, for a very long time.

So it was chance and coincidence which brought us to North London, Palmers Green, through the spontaneous generosity of family Konstantinowsky, and it was there that my new life in England started to unfold.

I shall not dwell on wartime England: enough has been said

and written about it. In spite of the Blitz, the Battle of Britain and wartime conditions, to me, age 15 and a half, it appeared like a land of milk and honey. Food rationing was fair and just, and after haphazard meals during our journey to England, eating was now a delight. But I was astounded to have thin bread and butter with fruit salad, to sample fruit jellies made with water, to hold the fork in a funny way, to eat an array of heavy puddings and custard and to have meat and vegetables smothered in gravy; and, horror of horrors, 'frog-spawn' – that is, tapioca pudding.

Clothing coupons were of no consequence to us because my parents couldn't afford to buy clothes. We existed on donations of clothes from the Red Cross and others, which my Mother and Ida altered, starched and laundered. But we were safe, together, free and well treated. Somewhere along the line I must have learnt English because I started school again, before Christmas 1940, six months after having left Paris. I started discovering London just as I had been exploring Paris. I knew all the buses which took me to a suitable tube station like Wood Green or Turnpike Lane and connections to go to the West End. Because of wartime security there were no maps available. That is why to this day I know pockets of London, rather than the whole of the city. Enough said, the new adventure of finding my way and getting to know yet another capital was quite revealing and enchanting.

School, Southgate County School, Palmers Green, was a very new experience. I met nothing but help and friendship on the part of staff and fellow pupils. The months and seasons went by, so did the war. I was completely engulfed and immersed in the 'Englishness' of my surroundings, English became 'my language' and London my home. There was a kind of normality, peace and continuity which I had not experienced in the previous few years, and this in spite of the course of World War II in bombed and dark London.

These were also my Mother's days of greatness. Out of nothing and with very little money she kept a home, in the two small rooms at Hedge Lane which was a real home, warm, secure, cosy, with wholesome food beautifully cooked on one small paraffin burner. Our clothes, the few that we owned, were clean and pressed. Of course I had to wear school uniform which was very new and strange to me. The navy blue gym tunic was in no way becoming and I disliked white masculine shirts with strangling ties, but perhaps it made dressing easier.

Betty Thackeray was my special friend and lived in Winchmore Hill, where I was often invited. She may have descended from the writer Thackeray. At any rate, she took it upon herself to introduce me to English literature, and lent and gave me several books. I still treasure her gift, *Anthology of English Poetry*.

Mother supplemented the small family income by making, or rather mass-producing, artificial flowers and leather belts. Also, once a week she had to trek to New Barnet Assistance Board, a long journey, to collect some additional allowance, I don't know on what grounds.

Father was restless. Because of his poor health he was not accepted for military service. He wanted to contribute to the war effort at all costs, but he was not received into the Medical Corps either. At that time doctors from other countries who had not got British qualifications were not allowed to practise medicine in Britain, so he could not work either. The London days, though challenging for Mother and quite thrilling for me, were indeed a frustration to him. Ever forceful and forward looking he made and renewed many personal and professional contacts, also with the Czechoslovak Government in exile, London. He read and studied widely, English in particular, making copious notes in his very own shorthand in the margins of books. I should mention that both my parents already had a fair command of English before arriving in this land. He decided to study for the British Medical Diploma, however long it would take. He also took it upon himself to help me with my school work, which at times I found tedious and I resented it thoroughly.

Nevertheless, with the passing of time, help and extra tuition from my teachers, persistent coaching from my Father and my own efforts, I managed to take the School Certificate

Examination exactly one year after starting at Southgate County School, and gained in December 1941 many fair grades and even a distinction in English language. Sadly, however, this was to be the end of my golden schooldays, at the age of 16 and a half.

No way could my parents afford to keep me at school, in spite of pressure from headmaster and staff. It was decided that I was to train as a secretary as quickly as possible, get a job, earn some money, and with my command of languages perhaps achieve something in that field.

Reluctantly I began at Hendon Technical College, London. Shorthand was fun and I took to it well and made good progress. But bookkeeping and so-called office practice left me cold. The worst, however, was typing. We were supposed to use all our fingers correctly, like playing the piano, touch-typing away, and this to the same dull tunes. The worst agony, and there I really got a glimpse of hell, was the typing pool where we were all together, perhaps 60 of us, and it seemed like hundreds, typing in assonance. I wanted to scream with anguish. At the end of six months I got my diploma and the job hunt began.

But in summer 1942 new legislation came out suddenly, no doubt because of wartime shortages: foreign doctors were now permitted to practise and work in British hospitals because apparently there were not sufficient British doctors left in civilian situations. Father bought the *British Medical Journal* and the *Lancet* weekly and wrote many applications, 100 to be exact, to a variety of hospitals up and down the country. My new found typing skills came useful, and I helped with his applications. He christened the replies 'sorry-spondence' because of all the refusals. These foreign doctors couldn't be trusted: in spite of the new laws there was endless prejudice.

At long last there was one reply, the 100th, and interview and acceptance followed. Father was appointed Assistant Medical Officer at Chartham Mental Hospital, near Canterbury, Kent: another vital landmark in our lives. We said 'farewell' to the Rabbies, moved ourselves and our few belongings to Chartham and took over part of a small house belonging to Mr and Mrs Hazelwood opposite the Mental Hospital entrance. They were a lovely old couple who almost looked alike, tending their garden and their polished, well-kept home. They marvelled with amazement at the explosions far and wide when bombs were dropped and they were spectators of the heavenly fireworks.

My Father suggested that I go back to school, to the sixth form, to continue my studies because he was now able to pay for my education. This I accepted with relief and pleasure.

I was to attend Simon Langton Girls' Grammar School, in the heart of ancient Canterbury, very near the cathedral. In September 1942 I dutifully went along, in my new compulsory school uniform complete with navy blue felt hat and yellow-maroon ribbon and registered for English, history, French and German to Higher School Certificate in two years' time. Somehow my studies never quite took off. There was something rigid, inflexible and unfriendly about my new surroundings. In the past I had always found it easy to make contact and assimilate but here it didn't seem to work. Even the English and history teachers were critical of my work without being helpful. Yet, 18 months before, I did not even speak a word of English. The culmination of what was oppressive to me was the strict obligatory school uniform and the dark blue hat. I repeatedly got into conflict with the headmistress through not wearing my hat. I was resentful of her and her small, limited horizons. She hadn't trekked down the dusty roads of France escaping from German armies.

When I was at my most depressed, the world fell to pieces again: Hitler's destructive bombardments of Canterbury seemed to come out of the blue. I was at Chartham and safe when most of the bombs fell and destroyed so much of the ancient city. There were renewed attacks and prospects of more. The school was closed for a brief time.

Father was a few paces ahead yet again in his thinking. He was concerned for my safety in Canterbury. He had also found out that in Britain a student could attend university on obtaining a good School Certificate, which I had got. He also understood that I was unhappy at Simon Langton School. So he asked me if I would like to go to university. My reply was immediate and in the affirmative. A letter was posted to the International Student Service and the British Council, London, containing my particulars, School Certificate and other documents. By return of post, in October 1942, I received admission to University College, Bangor, University of Wales – a free university place and two scholarships. My fate was sealed and I was to embark on the most important and far-reaching part of my life. With very little time lost, a few purchases such as a checked suit, skirt, navy blue jacket and two blouses, I was dispatched to Bangor, North Wales, changing at Crewe, and to my very new life. The university term had already begun.

I really meant to discuss 'nationhood'. Since our arrival in England in October 1940, citizenship did not preoccupy me, there was so much else. Life was so full. Of course the progress of the war was important to me but I was now less well-informed than in my early childhood; we were not in the thick of events any more, and my life was becoming peaceful, almost normal. My parents, however, had different thoughts. They sent Red Cross parcels and letters to the family in Hungary and received a few scanty replies. They were very concerned about them and their future. To me the past had receded and the present and future were all-important and had temporarily effaced the past. We had few contacts with the Czechoslovak government in exile, but all my new friends and contacts were English. To my knowledge my 'ex-government' had taken no notice of or interest in me personally and never granted educational or other help. England had really become my all-embracing home for the moment at any rate. I vaguely thought of returning home to Czechoslovakia, after victory, bringing with me my new found language skills. Now and again I was viewed as a curio amongst my university friends, expected to don national costume, leap onto a table and do a little native dance. This aspect of national labelling always upset me; I never had a national costume, I couldn't dance folk dances, nor sing. It was a label which did not fit me or my background, but one that well-meaning people who had never travelled beyond Dover and the White Cliffs, who had no notion about the Europe I had left, wanted to attach to the likes of me. To this day I am asked: What are you really? Czech, Hungarian, Slovak, French, Belgian, Austrian, English? From the preceding pages it may have become apparent that there is no clear answer, but that the self-imposed label 'central European' or just 'European' holds more truth.

The other recurring question which also grieved me and which I resented deeply was: How do you like England? I had no choice in the matter. England or more precisely Great Britain *happened*; it became my home. I was and still am thankful to be here and I did want to blend in, not to remain the eternal curio and outsider. My previous home or homes had become unattainable or non-existent. Home to me was always the place with my nearest and dearest, be it tent, caravan, room or palace. Is it coincidence that the first line of the Czechoslovak and now Czech anthem could indeed be my eternal refrain or question: *'Kde domov Můj?'* or 'Where is my home?'

News had spread to Bangor on the grapevine, before my arrival, that a 'Czechoslovak student' was to join the ranks. Bangor was very conscious of its nationhood, an aspect about which I knew nothing before my arrival. This was Wales, many of the students were Welsh speaking and certainly Welsh in their feelings, culture and background. I loved the sound of the Welsh language though I never came to master it, and my new friends and fellow students burst into song at all times. They were proud of their separateness, of their Welshness. At that time I did not understand the underlying political implications or notions of 'home rule'; I loved my new surroundings, the beautiful mountains and seashore, the mild climate and its lush vegetation. I was well received, probably more so because I was not English, and I made many good friends and was invited to many homes. I felt at home in Wales. Of course I had my special friends and together we discovered poetry, music, painting, life and men over cups of cocoa, by a small gas fire.

I enjoyed my studies, I threw myself into learning with delight and enthusiasm, perhaps because I had been deprived for so long. Independence, away from my parents' home, freedom and student life, were intoxicating. Yes, my four years at Bangor were the best years of my life!

Paradise was to be shattered suddenly. So was my allegiance to and love of my original homeland, Czechoslovakia, where I wished to return after the war, fully qualified and competent. Never before did I know of the existence of a Czechoslovak boarding school in Britain, near Shrewsbury, nor did the Czechoslovak government in exile ever question, advise or help in any way in my life or education since our arrival in October 1940. Suddenly I was presented with a *fait accompli* in the form of a registered letter: compulsion to complete my secondary education at the Czechoslovak school, as a boarder henceforth, or go to work in a munitions factory or join the army and leave Bangor immediately. This was spring 1943 and I was 17 and three quarters.

I would have been prepared to work or join the forces because I wanted Germany to be defeated and I wanted passionately that we should win the war. But truly, I could not understand the ultimatum, nor the reasons for going backwards educationally, back to school, to study in Czech for the Matura or Czech Baccalaureat, yet live in Great Britain where I had already obtained the English equivalents.

The matter was resolved: the Chancellor of the University of North Wales intervened, having sent a strong letter, together with comments from my lecturers and professors. I heard no more about the Czechoslovak school, and plunged back into my full and wonderful life and studies in Bangor, but my feelings towards my 'country of origin' were never the same again.

In fact, at the earliest opportunity, then at the age of 21, I applied for British citizenship, which was granted to me in November 1947 in Blackburn, Lancashire. The notary told me in all seriousness after I had attested and signed, that the chickens carved in wood adorning his mantelpiece were made in Czechoslovakia. I was married four months later and could have become 'British' by marriage but I wanted to become British by choice.

As the years go by and I proudly carry my well worn, faded navy blue British passport, my nomadic beginnings make me yearn for travel, to revisit familiar countries and pastures new. I can communicate in most lands, I am almost taken for a native in some. Truly, I belong nowhere totally, but I feel nearly at home in every land.

VI

The Childhood Diary

I found this linen-covered booklet, complete with padlock and key, in Stafford, England, amongst our belongings from the past, in 1947 when I was 22 years old, exactly ten years after my last entry on 1 July 1937. Here, I have translated everything from German into English, just as I found it, as I had written it when I was a child.

Let these unsophisticated words throw light on the world as it was then, seen by a young impressionable person, those years leading up to World War II, to our exodus and odyssey, which are really the subject of this book. May it serve as introduction to my story, the 'uncharted voyage'.

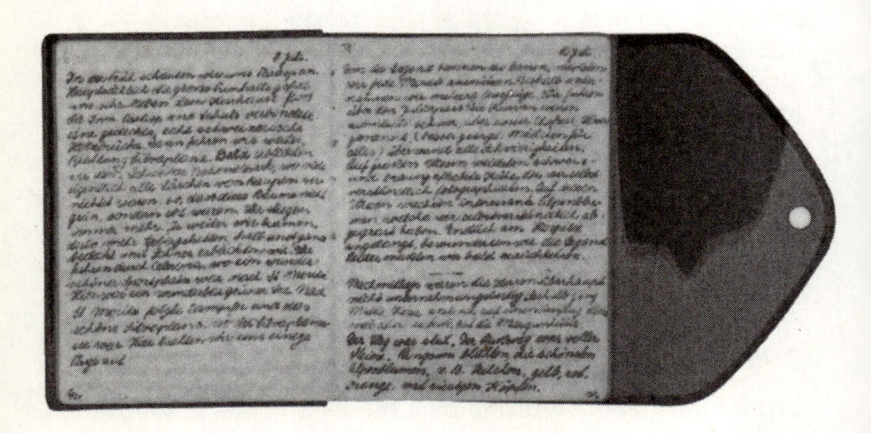

Calm before the storm

It was our last real summer holiday, one I remember particularly well. In July 1937, I was 12 years old, impressionable, a good traveller, but still a child enjoying childish pleasures and all of life. We still lived in a world of affluence.

My Father had never learnt to drive; so the expedition was a combined one with Mr Szalai (a friend and car owner), his car (a Fiat 12), his driver (Mr Kósa), my parents and me. The route was to be from Bratislava, then Czechoslovakia, through Austria, Switzerland and Italy and back through Austria, lasting about four weeks, without much previous planning or preparation. Once in Italy it became very hot and uncomfortable and there are no further diary entries, although I still recall the discomforts and highlights of this journey.

1 July 1937: my summer holidays (a verbatim translation from German)

At long last we left on July 1st, in the Fiat, or more exactly the old banger. Our first stop was Vienna where we spent a few hours. The onward journey was lonely, along the river Wachau, past Melk castle. At teatime we reached Amstetten and had tea in a smelly village café, the most important thing for our travel companion who often said: 'It may be smelly, but it's good'. Time passed quickly and at sunset we reached Gallspach, where professor Zeileis, homeopath and quack, as well as his son Dr Fritz lived and worked and practised healing. It was said that old Zeileis was 220 years old and treated the sick administering the same healing rays, whatever the disease, by exactly the same heat treatment. (My father pretended to be a patient, and so was admitted for treatment and observed all the hocus-pocus.)

2 July 1937

From Gallspach we drove past the wonderful Traun falls, to Gmunden where we stopped for lunch. After lunch, and a short break, to St Gilgen, on lake Wolfgang. On the other side of the lake you could see the charming White Horse Inn, as in the song, 'Im weissen Rössel am Wolfgangsee'. I wanted to bathe, but the water was rather cold and I wasn't allowed to swim. We drove along Lake Fuschl to Hallein, a lovely summer resort. The wild and wide river Salzach flows through Hallein, and could be seen from all the cafés. After tea, we drove over the first mountain pass, the Lueg. River Salzach accompanied us all the way, now far below in a deep ravine.

In the evening we arrived dead tired in Zell am See. Not only the lake site but also the town were so pretty and full of holidaymakers. In the evening it was lovely to see the illuminations like fairy lights all along the lake.

3 July 1937

An early start from Zell am See and on with the journey. We were now climbing and soon reached the summit of Thurnpass. From up above you could see the small houses in the valley looking like toys. In the Pass Hotel a huge St Bernard dog rushed to our welcome. After taking many photos and admiring the scene, we carried on. We were now in the land of Salzburg, and beyond the mountain pass lay the Tyrol. In the distance you could now see the snow-covered mountains, the Kitzbühel Alpine range, and we soon arrived in Kitzbühel itself. We particularly liked this town. Each ornate house was painted in different colours. After a good lunch, we carried on. It was terribly hot. We wanted to bathe in Jenbach, but there was no road leading down to the swimming pool, so we carried on and hoped for a dip in Innsbruck. We enquired, and a man on a bicycle led the way to show us the route to the '*Schwimmbad*'. Suddenly we heard a shriek, stopped and found we had run over a dog who had a broken leg. We carried on as quickly as possible, but didn't feel like bathing any more. A quick glance at the township, speedy afternoon tea and on to Seefeld where we were looking for accommodation.

4 July 1937

We wanted to stop in Seefeld for a few days' rest, a good choice. Seefeld was surrounded by high mountains and nearby was the lovely Wildsee (lake) where you could row and swim. We tried the water the next day. That is how a few lovely days went by, bathing, walking and playing with the animals in the Hotel. On the last day we went on an excursion to Oberleutasch and stopped at the inn called 'Zugspitze'.

7 July 1937

All good things have to come to an end and we had to leave Seefeld reluctantly. We drove to Innsbruck where we had to settle a few official matters, then back to Zirl through Imst where we were caught in a huge thunderstorm, through Landeck to Martinsbruck which was the Austro-Swiss frontier. So we reached a new country and to me an unknown foreign land. Landscape changed suddenly, but we still followed our faithful river Inn. Up in the mountains lay friendly little townships with steep, pointed church spires. Soon the winding Finstermünz Road emerged, full of beauty and interest. We drove along the route to Engadin until we reached Schuls Tarasp. There we stopped in the first inn, bought petrol and booked rooms for the night.

8 July 1937

In the morning we looked round Tarasp. We particularly liked the immense spa hall where guests took the waters. The river Inn flowed by the spa building. Tarasp and Schuls are linked by a typical Swiss covered wooden bridge. We then drove on, direction Silvaplana. We soon sighted the 'Swiss National Park' where many, in fact all large trees were destroyed by caterpillars, so that the trees were no longer green but had turned red. We were climbing higher and higher and saw more and more mountain ranges emerging, partly or completely covered in snow. We drove through Celerina, where I noticed a fabulous play and sports ground, then on to St Moritz by a wonderful deep green lake. Afterwards followed Campfer and lovely Silvaplana on lake Silvaplana. We stayed there for several days.

10 July 1937

We had to make the most of every moment to get to know this lovely region, so we made several excursions. We went up the Julierpass; the bends were fairly steep, but our driver Kósa (also called Jack of all trades) coped with all difficulties. In vast meadows black and brown spotted cows were grazing peacefully and of course we photographed them all. Most spectacular Alpine flowers were growing in these meadows and we picked bunches and bunches. A wonderful view from the summit but unfortunately we couldn't stay long. In the afternoon, the gentlemen weren't up to doing anything; so Mother, Kósa and I went on an excursion, on foot this time, up to the Margun hut. The path was steep and stony. Around us were the most beautiful Alpine flowers in full bloom, such as deep yellow, red and orange violets with immense heads and tiny stalks.

11 July 1937

Today we went on our best outing of all, up the Muottas Muraigl. We drove to Pontresina, the station in the valley and took the funicular, up to the height of 2,368 metres. Getting out of the funicular, the view from the top was marvellous. All of Engadin could be seen, the lakes of Campf, Pontresina, St Moritz, Silvaplana, Sils and Maloja. All around were snow-covered mountains. Now and again the mists receded and Piz Palü (4,002

Family photo 1921 - Back row left to right: Béla, Rosalie, Erwin. Front row left to right: Gisela. Jankus with baby Anny and Jónás

Paternal grandfather in Szeged

Maternal grandmother in Szeged

Gitta age 3

Gitta, writing at her desk in Bratislava

The garden at the house in Léva: Gisela, Rosalie, Anny and Gitta

Béla in the garden at Léva

'Are you Jewish, Gitta?' Gitta and Liesel

Gitta and Liesel in front of the theatre, Bratislava (1931)

Gitta dressed up as Bokros Birman (1933)

Year 2 at Bratislava Grammar School (1938)

8. Juli

In der Früh schauten wir uns Parsop an. Hauptsächlich die große Kurhalle gefiel uns sehr. Neben dem Kurhause floss die Inn. Parsop und Schuls verbindet eine gedeckte, echt schweizerische Holzbrücke. Dann fuhren wir weiter, Richtung Silvaplana. Bald erblickten wir den Schweizer Nationalpark, wo viele eigentlich alle Lärchen von Raupen vernichtet waren, so daß diese Bäume nicht grün, sondern rot waren. Wir stiegen immer mehr. Je weiter wir kamen, desto mehr Gebirgsketten, kahl und ganz bedeckt mit Schnee, erblickten wir. Wir fuhren durch Celerina, wo ein wunderschöner Sportplatz war, nach St. Moritz. Hier war ein wunderbar grüner See. Nach St. Moritz folgte Campfer und das schöne Silvaplana, wo der Silvaplanersee war. Hier hielten wir uns einige Tage auf.

10. Juli

Um die Gegend kennen zu lernen, mussten wir jede Minute ausnützen. Deshalb unternahmen wir mehrere Ausflüge. Wir fuhren über den Julierpass. Die Kurven waren ziemlich schwer, aber unser Chafeur, Rosa gennant, (besser gesagt: Mädchen für alles) überwand alle Schwierigkeiten. Auf großen Wiesen weideten schwarz- und braungefleckte Kühe, die wir selbstverständlich fotografierten. Auf diesen Wiesen wuchsen interessante Alpenblumen, welche wir selbstverständlich abgerast haben. Endlich am Hospitz angelangt, bewunderten wir die Gegend. Leider mussten wir bald zurückkehren.

Nachmittags waren die Herren überhaupt nicht unternehmungslustig, deshalb ging Mutti, Rosa, und ich auf einen Ausflug, diesmal aber zufuss, auf die Margunhütte. Der Weg war steil. Der Aufstieg war voller Steine. Ringsum blühten die schönsten Alpenblumen, z.B. Nelken, gelb, rot, orange, mit riesigen Köpfen.

A page from my original diary

Skiing in the Czech mountains with Gretl (February 1937)

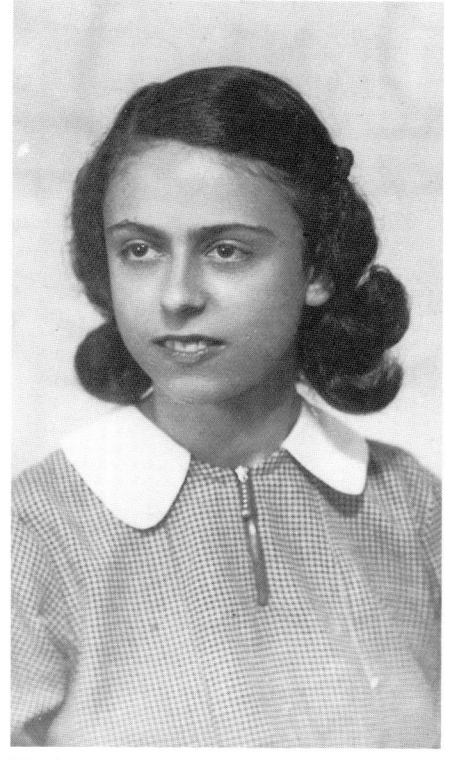

The last days in Bratislava, harder times

Last glimpse of Bratislava and the Danube

Gitta, the university student

The intrepid travellers, Erwin and Rosalie

Seaton Library

Phone enquiries: 0345 155 1001
www.devonlibraries.org.uk

Borrowed Items 16/02/2023 15:33
XXXXXXXXXX1475

Item Title	Due Date
Uncharted voyage : a wartime saga.	09/03/2023
Sailing the dream : the amazing true story of the	09/03/2023
Behind closed doors : the tragic, untold story of	09/03/2023

Friends of Seaton Library (FoSL)
Join the FoSLs for just £1 per year and help support your local library

EVENTS

Support your local library - Libraries Unlimited, registered charity number; 1170092

BOUNCE RHYME
Join us every Wedensday from 9:30 for a sing song and boogie at our Bounce Rhyme sessions.

Erwin and Rosalie, Bratislava 1936

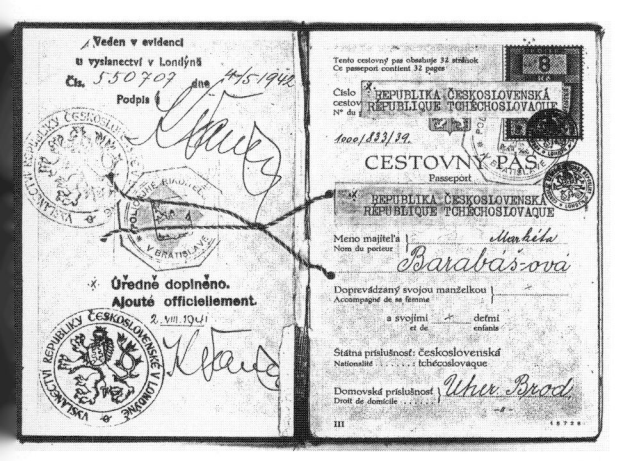

Czechoslovakian passport

Spanish frontier closed

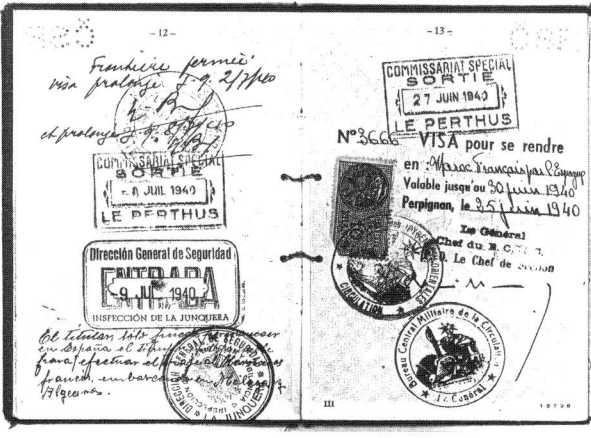

Gitta and family in Birmingham, 1959. Front row left to right: Penny, Gitta, Lesley, Alison, Michael, Christopher, Robert behind

Family gathering in Germany, 1963. Front row left to right: Lesley, Gitta, Michael, Rosalie, Anny, Penny, with Christopher in front, Alison at the back

metres high) would show its white peak. Cameras and binoculars were working away! We walked on and came to a meadow covered in snow and a wild snowball fight followed. Finally we got back to the mountain railway and descended to Silvaplana. We drove northward over Fluella Pass until Zernez. In this friendly little town there were only houses painted white and even the church was snow-white. Fluella Road got narrower and narrower and you had to drive through many tunnels. It was always a catastrophe when two cars met. Below flowed a stream, certainly full of gushing glacier waters. Over this stream were bridges, but not iron or wooden ones but bridges formed of frozen snow. This marvel did surprise me. The higher we got, the lonelier and more desolate it became. Nothing but rock and snow... The road seemed to drag, bends became steeper and almost rectangular. Finally we reached the Pass summit.

There are photographs and memories, but no further entries about this journey in the diary. Many years later I marvel at my carefree life. Perhaps I haven't changed so much, my personality was already formed: I still revel in travel, beauty, bathing and people. I notice that most of this diary is written in the first person plural, the 'we' form. Also, although I have checked the route and spelling of geographical terms I found everything to be surprisingly accurate and correct.

School, my beloved school

The next entry is written 17 months later. I was then 13 and a half years old and there had already been many political and human changes. I am now a teenager, confused and apprehensive about the world and school, still writing in German, though attending the 4th year form of a Slovak Girls' grammar school (Dievčenský gymnasium) in central Bratislava, where the teachers, men and women, were Czechs and Slovaks.

A general 'mobilisation' calling up all able-bodied men had been announced a few weeks before the Treaty of Munich in September 1938 when general war was feared and expected. After the Munich settlement of 29 September 1938, there was so-called 'peace', but in fact there was anxiety, demoralisation, partition of lands and a general exodus. This meant 'ethnic cleansing': Czech speaking citizens returned to Czech lands and Moravia; a part of Slovakia became part of Hungary. Banská Bystrica, the centre of Slovakia, became the focal point of Slovakia and the seat of the new 'Hlinka Government', a puppet regime. Austria, barely 20 kilometres away, was under Nazi Germany. Jews feared the future. These events were the fundamental reasons for upheavals in school management and everyday life and the premonitions of an ominous future.

4 December 1938

I haven't written in my diary for a very long time, I haven't even completed the beautiful holiday journey. Since then a lot has happened, another summer has gone. This time holidays inland Slovakia, in the Tatra mountains and not abroad. We have lived through a general military mobilisation, Father had to be soldier for one week. They were frightening days, full of excitement and uncertainty and other political happenings.

From now on I shall note down everything carefully in order to remember the present times.

Not only the world has turned upside down but school as well. My favourite teachers, my favourite fellow pupils are gone! The day before yesterday we learnt that our form teacher Löblová was to be transferred to Banská Bystrica. We were devastated. The darling of our 'gymnasium' must leave! We pupils of 4A were afraid that we might not even be able to say goodbye to her before she left and that is why we created such a scene. We just wanted to see her once more. Kostlivá, another teacher, was such a sport, she found out Löblová's whereabouts; but she was not allowed to come into our classroom. We were beyond ourselves with rage. Two pupils had bought a box of chocolates and a bunch of roses on our behalf and finally handed the gifts over to Löblová outside the staffroom. She cried and embraced the girls.

The whole class was still distraught. After gymnastics we were to have French. We all ran out into the corridor when Dibelka (another teacher due to leave the school) also said goodbye to us. We were now racing about wildly all over the place, excited and out of control and made a terrible noise. We waited a little longer to see if Löblová would emerge but really thought the new headmaster would not allow her to be seen. That is why we shouted, at the top of our voices, like real demonstrators: 'My chceme Löblovú, my chceme Löblovú...' (We want Löblová...). Finally Triska (new deputy head teacher) appeared, he seemed to have been offended by the noise and went straight to the headmaster to complain about our form (4A). A moment later Triska appeared with the new headmaster Lisý, white with rage, he could have beheaded us all. He thought ours was a political reaction, that is why he was so furious, apprehensive and literally threw us out of school. 'OK' we said to ourselves, gathered outside the school entrance, shouted even louder and as loud as we could. Ulehla (the old headmaster) and Prokesová came out. Ulehla, though now replaced by the new head, understood us. With tears in his eyes he spoke to us, promised to send Löblová to see us and ordered us back into school, and we obeyed. On the stairs stood Löblová hardly recognisable, pale, ruffled, red-eyed and she said: 'Girls, go back to the classroom, you are only making it hard for yourselves. Behave quietly so that things can be settled. I'll come and see you tomorrow at break.' I shall never forget that sad moment.

We went back to class and there followed an interrogation. At 12 o'clock we were all sent home. The matter was reported in the press.

Perhaps everything will change again one day for the better. I do hope so...

We always celebrated St Nicholas (Mikuláš) Day on 6 December and received small gifts of sweetmeats. The festive colours were red and black. St Nicholas is a Father Christmas figure.

6 December 1938, 'Mikuláš'

And still more things have happened. St Nicholas Day has been and gone. It took me a long time before deciding, according to old custom, to put my shoes into the window on December 5th, the night before. Next morning I did in fact find them as always, filled with birch twigs, red and black little toy devils, sweets, nuts and mandarin oranges. I am glad that there were fewer presents this year, times are so bad and with the money clothes could have been bought for a needy child, so much more necessary than a toy for me.

The baptism

There were many baptisms of 'convenience' at the time after Munich and before the outbreak of World War II. It was hoped that becoming 'Christian' would save Jewish lives and be accepted by Nuremberg race laws, in the wake of growing anti-Semitism. I was confused but took my baptism very seriously, and tried to abide by the new teachings. A bitter experience in the confessional, however, when I was 13 and a half years old, when I really had nothing to confess, destroyed all my illusions about Catholicism.

7 December 1938

Today was our baptism. Mass began at 8 in the morning but Imi (the priest) was late. Rosa was my godmother. I imitated everything she did. In spite of myself I had to giggle when I saw Imi in his robes and black cap. Baptism followed Holy Mass. We went into a small room called Sacristy, I think. Imi changed into special robes and then it was our turn. He blessed us, poured holy water on us, made the sign of the cross, sprinkled salt onto our lips and said many prayers for us. Again I copied all gestures which Rosa, Mother and Father made as well. I had to laugh when the priest said a few incomprehensible Latin words to us.

All laughter vanished when I thought of Rosa who had been godmother in the very same room before, for little Franzl ... whose mother (Rosa's sister) died in childbirth, and the baby soon afterwards. This was only a hollow ceremony, I remain a non-believer; fortunate those who believe! If only I had been brought up with some religion, life would be so much easier to bear...

We said a few more prayers at the main Altar, we were then given holy wafers (communion), Imi wished us well and dismissed us.

The next thing to do was breakfast after fasting, so on to the next best café called Regina. I don't know why I suddenly felt merry and exuberant whilst the grown-ups were discussing today's events and affairs. Then I suddenly felt sad. What an important day this has been, not really for me, but for my documents and personal papers. Perhaps baptism will have helped to save us after all in time to come!

The beginning of the end

My Father went to Paris on a return ticket from Prague in March 1939 to meet his Hungarian cousin's husband, General Georges Gayet, in order to discuss possibilities of work and life in one of the French colonies. The day of his return, on the way to the airport on 15 March 1939, he bought a newspaper which had the headlines 'Hitler marches into Prague'. He decided, therefore, to stay in Paris and not return home. 'I am the first refugee', he said to himself. He did everything in his power to arrange for Mother and me to follow on to

France, he was in constant touch with us and feared the worst: a complete occupation of Czechoslovakia with persecutions to follow and that is why he insisted on us coming as soon as possible. We finally joined him eight months later, in October 1939. In the following diary pages I talk about the months of separation before our final departure. The scenario is Father in France, Mother and I in Bratislava (by then Hlinka dominated Slovakia), grandparents and family in Hungary, doing everything possible to prevent us from leaving. The Hungarian relatives felt that we were breaking up the family, that we were guilty of leaving them in the lurch. My poor Mother was truly confused and between two fires.

Flowers and leatherwork

Mother was convinced that she would have to be breadwinner once abroad. That is why she learnt leathercraft and how to make flower fashion accessories.

31 March 1939

The world has gone topsy-turvy once more, and so have I. We went to Budapest for New Year. Anny and I had a few words together in secret, in the evening. She was telling me about love. Because of her race (born of Jewish parents) she couldn't marry the Hungarian officer she was engaged to. True, I don't have any feeling for them (the Hungarian Military), but she should have known what she wanted. Also she is ill. I fear for her life. She is the only person in the world in whom I have one hundred percent confidence. We also talked about religion. She asked me about my views. I told her straight that I believed in nothing. She tried to explain: who would have created the world? Who could have ordered all so wonderfully if not God? She wanted to convert me to Christianity. For the time being she suggested I said the Lord's Prayer every night. I did so for a while... Anny had converted me just a little. From then on I prayed now and again in the evening and told God my wishes... I prayed for my Father so that he may thrive and prosper in Paris. But I did not ask for his return, I left that decision in God's hands. Probably Father will remain abroad and we (Mother and I) should follow. It is so sad without him, prayer is my only consolation. If only we could see him soon again! I think my Grandparents (Mother's parents) are angry with him because he is 'taking us away from them'. If only the whole family were united and at one! Mother seems to be getting weaker and weaker. I fear that she might not be able to stand the terrible strain of packing, removals and leaving. School is a burden to me now. I sit down with my books, all good intentions but I start to think and think...

If only we were there already! Nothing draws me to Bratislava any more, neither wealth, comfort nor friends. I would miss nothing, if only we were together again as a family. May God protect us all!

28 April 1939

Now we really are preparing for the journey. But everything drags out just like a sausage. I really am in a strange frame of mind, my restlessness is acute. I can see that Mother has a great deal to do, but I don't consider that she is doing enough. When she sits down to her flower-making (fashion accessories) I am furious because she really ought to be doing something else, something much more important towards our departure. But when I consider we may possibly have to live on her earnings making flowers when we are abroad, I feel ashamed. I almost explode with anger when she won't let me help with anything. Then she is angry too when I make a scene. Out of fury and desperation, I could jump out of the window there and then. A little later when I have calmed down, and have come to my senses, I realise how stupid I had been, lecturing or rushing her, I know that I only hold her up and make it more difficult for her. When progress is too slow and I grumble, I am only offending her yet again. And she could fall ill, may God preserve us. I could jump out of the window, or open the gas tap, but I do see again how ridiculous this would be. Only more worry for my parents, and I would commit a great sin... Perhaps after all somewhere, sometime, beautiful life is awaiting me. I try to calm down but don't find comfort at all. I don't have friends. Why can't I find a suitable friend when others can? Why can't I find any enjoyment or entertainment when others do? Am I different? More stupid, more serious, more depressive and melancholy than the others. I have never shared serious secrets with Gretl, but I have always felt she was an honest, open friend. Now she is friends with Elfi and we have become more estranged. I hate Elfi, I don't know why. Kitty is false. Yet we do talk together, also about sex, birth and relationships but I can't find a complete answer or solution. Others are in the know. I am ashamed and dare not ask Mother or Anny.

Shall I ever see Anny again? I was so sad when we said farewell (New Year). Perhaps we shall meet again some day. My dear diary, I am asking you questions, in vain, questions about the secrets of nature, questions about life and our future, I don't know what lies before me, when we can leave, when we can join my beloved Father again. Perhaps I am blind towards him because I love him so much, even more now that he is far away. I think Mother is hurt because she feels I prefer him...

5 August 1939

Omi (grandmother) was here. She was very excited and worried about us. But I don't really like her any more. She has false eyes. Perhaps I am wrong, but this is my impression. She is terribly upset that we are leaving. Stupid, but what can you do? I am really angry with her and there is one thing I'll never forget: they were talking about the possibility of us going to Budapest or Léva before travelling to Paris. Omi insists that we should do so, at all cost. Mother was to convalesce with them for a few weeks. Father is totally against it, in his letter and on the phone he says that we should come earlier, as early as possible, before there is something to prevent it. He really has good reasons to insist, I know for certain, it is not just a selfish wish. I remarked that Father had written, saying that we should come as soon as possible, without paying heed to trifles. Omi replied in a sarcastic tone of voice, 'It is certainly urgent for *him*'. She (Omi) should have realised it wasn't for *him*, but for *our* well-being. I was livid. I left the room, threw myself onto my bed and began to sob, inconsolably. Grief and anger subsided gradually. Life is so strange, slowly you forget even the most acute pain. If only I could get away from here with Mother as quickly as possible and join Apu (Father). And if only both of them could get along well together without arguments! I wouldn't care how we lived, even if we were poor, if only we could live happily together again in peace.

There are no further entries.

VII

Cameos From the Past

Leucate, 29 March 1995

I have just read, spellbound, Thomas Kenealy's *Schindler's List*. The story is totally relevant and related to my own story. I am fortunate not to have been one of the 'Auschwitz Children', nor one of the 'Schindler Women', but I might have been. I have escaped their fate, but I retain deep emotional rapport and feeling for them, and their shadow is never far away.

Reading this book evoked memories of their survival and mine, at times pathetic, incongruous and far-fetched. Some incidents triggered off images and moments long forgotten, pebbles of a monumental survival.

Official papers, forged and otherwise

Birth certificates, as they were issued in central Europe and Czechoslovakia at the time of my parents' birth and mine, included the usual factual headings of time, place and names, but also the stigma of religion, information used or abused to the full in Hitler's Europe. Therefore, my '*Rodný List*' (birth certificate) said clearly under the heading '*náboženstvo*' (religion): Israelské (Jewish). There was similar information on my parents' certificate, but in Hungarian. Thus, in an era of Jew-cleansing and anticipating the 'final solution', such a certificate could have meant a direct train to Auschwitz.

I referred in Chapter VI to the christening or baptism of my parents and myself – life-saving baptisms of convenience as conceived by them, an act of devotion and sincerity and subsequent disappointment for me.

So, after the baptism of our family we were issued with baptismal certificates, proving the fact of a changed religion. Perhaps that piece of paper may have been one step towards avoiding our fate, but no guarantee because it still referred to our Jewish birth.

As in *Schindler's List* there were numerous document forgers or legal document alterers in Bratislava. Through the grapevine my Father knew how to set about obtaining forged papers. Some official was located who out of kindness or for profit or probably both, mass-produced new, authentic-looking birth certificates, complete with numerous authentic-looking official stamps (*Kolok*), dated the day of baptism. The section 'Religion' clearly stated 'Roman Catholic', with all other details as on the original certificate. Therefore, at a glance, the offending information 'Jewish' did not figure, and on the face of it the document was complete and correct. My parents and I were now the proud owners of laundered non-Jewish birth certificates and the original ones conveniently disappeared.

Ironically, when my birth certificate needed to be produced again, we had arrived in England after our wartime odyssey. On English certificates there was no column for religion, therefore the 'Roman Catholic' information did not impress anyone and in fact I never divulged the story of my baptism.

Over 50 years later when I returned to Bratislava, my home town, for the second time, with my little companions, Krystina and Simona, we went to the 'Rodný Úrad' (Registry for Births and Deaths) in a narrow street of the old city, opposite 'Kapučinský Kláštor'. The officer in charge turned out to be a rotund, smiling blonde lady, so different from the officialdom I learnt to dread and fear in my childhood days. I explained in my hesitant Slovak, yet with a nearly perfect accent, that I had lost my original certificate and wanted a replacement. The lady was mystified, asked a few questions and produced the

1925 *Book of Entries* and made an extract for me for the colossal sum of 7 crowns (a few pence). She asked if I wanted to see the relevant section in the book, which I did, of course. There, in my Father's handwriting, dated a few days after my birth (August 1925) were all the family details and his signature. It seemed like ghosts of the past. There was also an entry concerning the date and nature of our conversion to Roman Catholicism. But the new certificate issued had no reference to the Jewish or any other religion because the present format no longer called for it. Times have changed.

Money, thrift and clothes

I received no pocket money and was told to just ask, but I never did, proud even then! I said before that in the good pre-war years, before events leading up to the Munich crisis, we lived well. There were no obvious shortages and money was rarely discussed. But there was a general aura of thriftiness which I disliked and resented. Twice a year, a dressmaker would move in for a few days before the onset of winter and again before summer, to sew or more particularly, to work on alterations. I mentioned before that my maternal grandparents had a draper's store in Levice, and many a length of special fabric was put on one side by my grandmother. Garments were always made of very good material, which meant that they were to be used again and again, though brought up to date and made more fashionable. How I resented those everlasting navy and white serge clothes of extra special quality made into yet another garment for yet another season. It was all so dull and of such wonderful quality and I so longed for the gaudy and shabby more youthful fashions. Another plight was the fact that I was allergic to wool, one of my earliest childhood memories. Grandfather brought me a bright orange and yellow long-sleeved knitted dress from Prague: he must have understood that I longed for colour, that I dreaded the sensible. Being only little, I was put on a table facing the big mirror to try on Prague's latest children's fashions. I stretched both my arms out horizontally in anguish and screamed: the fabric made me itch, cry and ache. So one of the seasonal dressmaker's tasks was to line all my winter clothes. I hated the mothball smell of fabric, cottons and unwashed bearded ladies which lingered during their days of residence.

How fellow travellers helped one another

As with 'Schindler's children', so with the refugees who came over to England with us. There was a great sense of belonging and mutual help, as I have not experienced before nor since. That meant that those members of the 'club' who settled and came into some money or belongings before the others, immediately offered thoughtful and generous gifts to the less fortunate.

It so transpired that Eduard Erdelyi, known by all as Eduardo, an ex-veteran anti-Franco soldier of the Spanish Civil War, a bachelor with curly black hair and animated gestures, haunted my parents throughout our 'odyssey' and I deeply resented his continuous presence for no logical reason. He was an electrical engineer by training, and the very first of our group to obtain work, at Vickers Armstrong, Weybridge, Surrey – work much related to the war effort. His first gesture after receiving his first pay packet was to rent a radio for my parents, a gift never to be forgotten and eternally appreciated. The next person to find a foothold in London was Otakar Kraus, an opera singer by training, listed in the *Oxford Dictionary of Music*. He sang baritone with the Carl Rosa Opera Company, Covent Garden, and also at European festivals. He gained an OBE before his death. When in prison in Portugal with us (Forte Caxias, Lisbon), he was the self-appointed music director of our group of 'prisoners' who were walked back from the gardens to the dormitories along the long stone-carved tunnels. He led the chant of the 'Volga Boatmen' in his bass-baritone, with everyone joining in, and I can still hear the echo of the voices in my head.

It was Otakar and his wife, Mana, who showed the deepest

understanding for the likes of me, then aged 16, a young girl uprooted but not distressed, and clothed in Red Cross donations and other charity offerings, though beautifully laundered and maintained by my Mother. They invited me to their flat, off Tottenham Court Road, London, in order to go shopping for clothes with them, something which in spite of our apparent affluence in the past I had never experienced. I can still see the shop in wartime bomb-blitzed London, on the left-hand side of Tottenham Court Road, walking away from Marble Arch. There I was allowed to choose, and I selected a soft, warm, tomato-red dress, with a braided Peter Pan collar and long, slightly puffed sleeves. I was young, dark, with a high colouring and felt wonderful in my first new dress. When I got home to Palmers Green, 142 Hedge Lane, I unwrapped the parcel excitedly to show my Mother. She took one look and said: 'Couldn't you have chosen a sensible navy blue?' I think I cried for a long time.

Otakar made a name for himself and appeared in several early productions of Benjamin Britten's operas, some at the Theatre Royal, Birmingham, a theatre long gone. We went to all the productions, for the sake of Otakar, and also because of the newly discovered and loved music of Britten. Otakar came to visit us at home, in Harborne, Birmingham, but I really forget the details.

Every moment of my childhood and war years is crystal clear in my mind, but once normality and relative peace followed, impressions, years and events have merged and diffused. Yes, Otakar Kraus was perhaps the most famous of our fellow travellers, not to forget my contact with Ján Masaryk, the first Czechoslovak president's famous son.

To provide for the future

I am returning to the wheeling, dealing and buying, Schindler style. Back in October 1939, soon after the Treaty of Munich, it was evident that we would be leaving sooner or later, destination unknown, and that money would become valueless.

In any case, we would not be allowed to take money out of the country. Therefore, ways had to be found to convert money (*Koruny*) into things and investments which would hold their value, be transferable, portable, desirable, convertible and saleable. The grand spending spree had started, with foresight and at the same time tremendous recklessness. We would have to provide for ourselves for eternity with our belongings, because we might never again be able to earn or possess money. We would have to sell or barter so as not to die of starvation, a childish simplification perhaps. Then after Munich with the ultimate declaration of war, the end of the world seemed round the corner.

The first purchase I recollect at the age of 14, towards my 'trousseau', was a china teaset. The notion of marriage seemed irrelevant if not ridiculous, but buying beautiful things, given the choice, and just spending money were fun. The notion of the unknown was fun too, though I knew it would be in bad taste to admit my delight. I chose a delicate, thin, pale blue china teaset with narrow white rims, made in Czechoslovakia. I think the cost was 250 crowns (*koruny*). The shop is no longer in Venturská Ulica – I looked for it nostalgically in 1994. The china teaset is still with me. I don't use it, it is not suitable for the dishwasher, but I gaze at it when I open my sideboard and approve of my choice and taste of over 56 years ago!

Gold

Gold coins were always a coveted commodity, in times of pogroms, wars or revolutions. They were small enough to handle and hide, stable enough to hold or increase in value. So when eavesdropping on numerous hushed adult conversations, I gathered that bank accounts were to be emptied (you could never trust a bank) and gold was to be purchased, for coin as well as gold value. I never knew when, where nor how. Gold in our family jargon was christened 'Olga' – 'O' for 'Or' in French, and 'Olga' also became synonymous with money. It was necessary to prepare a secret code language for the ominous future. All these preparations fitted in with my reading of Mark Twain's novels (in German or Slovak translation), but real life promised to be more exciting than books. 'You must never put all your eggs in one basket' was the gospel I heard again and again, and even now I still abide by that principle. I think some gold was buried in my grandparents' garden in Levice; I don't know if it was ever recovered or not.

A considerable number of coins were placed inside my 'head', to be found again and recovered in 1947. There was an artist and sculptor, named Bokros Birman who was a patient of my Father's and a frequent visitor to Konventná 17. I found him comical and intriguing beyond measure. One day I dressed up in my Father's overcoat and trilby and impersonated him in my version of Hungarian, selling prints, books and pictures. This brought the house down and I remember the incident more through photographs. When I was about 5 years old, Bokros made a bronze plaque of my profile and this was subsequently mounted onto an oak plinth. When departure and danger became imminent in 1938, it was decided to unscrew the plinth, place gold coins inside the plaque and screw it up again (I knew nothing of the operation). That is how the coins in my head spent and survived the war and emerged again in England in 1947.

Another package of gold coins, many Olgas, had a stickier time during the war years. A cylindrical metal sweet tin was found, I think the make was 'Heller'. Intermingled with the coins were fruit drops; in fact there were many more coins than sweets. This was placed in our emergency picnic basket and the tin travelled with us throughout the flight from France to England. It was considerably lighter by the time we got to England on 28 October 1940. I don't know about any of the transactions, but even in the worst days, Olga must have come to our rescue.

The stone

Then came the story of the stone, 'Dr Stein' in family jargon, a large investment diamond which was supposed to save the day. I don't know where or how the worthy doctor hibernated during the war years. When he came to me after my Mother's death and I decided that I was not interested in diamond rings, I preferred to convert him into a flight ticket to some remote island. I hate transactions and am not good at them. Of course the stone was not perfect, of course the value of diamonds at that moment in time was low, and really there was little demand. I wanted to be rid of the doctor and the proceeds of the sale allowed me to travel as far as Australia.

The removal

But the story of stories is how we dispatched the contents of surgery and apartment from Bratislava, Konventná 17, just before World War II, late in August 1939, and found everything again, intact, without a broken cup, in the spring of 1947, in Stafford, England.

I referred earlier to the grand money-spending spree. This went on for quite a while, right up to the dispatch of our goods and chattels, all to provide for rainier days, wherever...

My Father was already in Paris, having left home a week before the occupation of Prague in March 1939. Though abroad and absent, he was undoubtedly 'Master of Ceremonies' and 'Master Brain' of our planned escape, destination unknown.

The war was imminent and we were to pack and dispatch everything, grand piano included, to Boulogne-Sur-Mer, France, a convenient seaport for further dispatch. I shall never forget the two enormous wooden containers holding and gobbling up the total contents of home and surgery. When the load finally departed, my childhood home was bare and hollow. We were left with mattresses on the floor, table and chairs, personal luggage, my little leather suitcase and nothing else. The grand adventure had started. But little did we know...

Very soon after the transport's arrival in France, war had broken out. Seaports were for the exclusive use of the military and all civilian loads and transports had to be moved inland, away from prospective military zones. By September 1939, my Father was residing in Vichy, central France, notorious later as the capital of 'unoccupied' Vichy France. So it made sense for him to give Vichy as a forwarding address, care of the removal firm Brancher. At that point in time, my Mother and I were somewhere between Bratislava and Budapest.

We had no further contact with our belongings. I don't know whether my parents had paid any storage moneys during our life in France until June 1940. I assume that there may have been some communication or even financial settlement.

When France fell in June 1940, we were on the run, for real, with thousands of other refugees along the roads of France, heading for Spain; we only wanted to save our skin and never gave belongings any thought. We continued our voyage (the story told in the diaries) and finally arrived and settled in England in October 1940, at the height of the Blitz, where we lived during the war years. My parents had created and furnished a small home, having arrived in England with no possessions at all.

After the war, in 1947, my Father decided, out of the blue, to send a letter to Vichy, addressed to Monsieur Brancher, of the removal firm, to enquire if they knew anything of the whereabouts of the two containers, sent in 1939. Much to everyone's surprise, the prompt reply was as follows: 'Both lift vans are still in storage in Vichy'. We had several choices: to forget about the whole affair; or to go to Vichy, pay seven years' storage, collect a few items and dispose of the rest; or to have both containers sent to England, pay seven years' storage as well as transport from France to England.

For better or for worse, my parents took the last option and awaited arrival of the mammoth transport. Father was then working as a doctor at Stafford Mental Hospital and the isolation hospital wing adjoining their dwelling stood empty at the time and could be used for storage.

On arrival, everything was unpacked, unscathed. It was like a three-dimensional surrealist apparition from the past. The overwhelming feature was size: central-European spaciousness within English matchbox-sized dwellings. Much had to be sold, given away or discarded. But my parents were once more surrounded by their familiar objects, which after nearly nine years they had learnt to live without. From that point on they would be slaves to the past. Only houses and accommodation large enough to take the gigantic bookcase, sideboards, king-size beds, banqueting tables and so forth, would be acceptable. They had a retirement bungalow built in Stafford to fit the dimensions of the furniture. But my Father died in 1961, just before they were due to move in.

So my Mother came to Birmingham instead, to be near us, to an apartment large enough to house some of her giants. But she was happy to be surrounded by memories of the past and she was at peace amongst them, particularly in the last years of her life.

A few chosen objects are with me still. The dining table is one where I sat as a little girl, where we all sat right up to August 1939 and talked and talked and talked. 'Where can we go? Where shall we be safe?' The very same table in my dining room is where we have family meals, or dinners with friends, and they all, except for the little children, are reluctant to leave the table.

Foresight and planning

Foresight was probably the key to our survival. I have acquired and retained this instinct and still like to be a few paces ahead of every happening.

I am now in Switzerland, in the summer of July 1937, the best and last pre-war holiday abroad. We travelled by car, a stylish, ancient Fiat 12, the owner and handsome driver Mr Kósa, my parents and I. We stayed in a motley of hotels, some shabby, some not. We were on the move, we climbed mountains and picked Alpine flowers. I was in my element. I did not appreciate the decadent or swansong nature of things, nor the imminent dangers during that glorious summer of 1937. My Father knew, of course, and without my knowledge (but I heard later) he deposited a sum of money in a Swiss bank. Later this was to be my Father's salvation when he was alone and penniless in Paris, after the German occupation of Prague. In addition, two weekly letters from Bratislava to Paris, containing five-crown postal coupons, convertible to French francs, were sent by my Mother without fail. These also helped my Father to survive in the first months of being a refugee.

The escape route

Emigration had preoccupied my parents for several years and the need for a decision became more important with the rise of Hitler. It was chance and coincidence which triggered off everything.

My Father had a Hungarian first cousin, Lili, once a very beautiful girl, or so the story goes. When a French army detachment reached Szeged in 1920, after the Treaty of Trianon, a handsome French officer, called Georges Gayet, spotted her, fell in love with her, and they married in Budapest with pomp and circumstance. They then settled in France and the French colonies and had four children. Georges Gayet's army career was brilliant and he became a general. I believe a statue has been erected to him in Madagascar.

In despair because there was little hope on the horizon, Father contacted Georges and Lili at their Paris address, perhaps in February 1938, with a view to meeting Georges, in order to discuss the possibilities for a Czechoslovak doctor (my Father) to work in a French colony, however remote. A meeting was arranged, Father went to Paris, but the day of his return flight to Prague, Hitler had already occupied the capital of Czechoslovakia and my Father remained in France, the first unplanned refugee. I don't know anything about the outcome of the meeting between them, but Georges Gayet remained our guardian angel, in the background, throughout our exile on French soil.

Irony of fate

My maternal grandparents were very distressed about our emigration to France and did everything in their power to delay my Mother's and my final departure: we were breaking up the family! They did not see the course of events clearly and there seemed to be a misleading respite and false lull in Hungary, where they lived at that time.

Grandfather (Opi to me) financed Béla's (Father's brother and Anny's father) journey to Paris, some time between April and July 1939 for a sole purpose and mission: to convince my Father that there was no danger at home (in Czechoslovakia or Hungary) and to plead with him to return as soon as possible, for the sake of the family. It was wrong and cruel, they implied, to have left home, to insist that Mother and I were to follow and to split the family.

Father was emphatic in his reply to his elder brother, but he would stay on in Paris and insisted that Mother and I should follow as soon as possible because of the political shape of things to come; and that indeed, brother Béla, for his own safety, should remain in Paris there and then. But Béla returned to Budapest, was taken away with other 'Jews' and journalists, and was last heard of in Kecskemét, Hungary, in April 1944, then never again, having disappeared without a trace. His name and dates are now engraved onto one of the leaves of the sculpted Martyrs' willow tree in the Memorial Gardens of Budapest Synagogue.

Both grandparents, together with other relatives from Léva-Levice, left in one of the last railway wagons, in April 1944, to Auschwitz concentration camp. Their death was confirmed in a Red Cross notification, addressed to my parents in Stafford, in 1945, after the end of the war in Europe. The names of Jónás and Gisela Blumenthal are engraved into the marble Holocaust Memorial at the Jewish cemetery, Budapest. This news was horrendous. I understood some of the implications in 1945. But in 1945 I lived life to the full, far from hell, which we had left behind. I began to grasp my Mother's grief and sadness later with the passing of time. I understand the horror of it all more deeply as I grow older. The Holocaust had killed my beloved grandparents. My children and grandchildren, the children after them – they must never forget.

VIII

The Wartime Diary (The Flight)

Introduction

The time has come to write about my odyssey, the flight from the advancing German forces, the flight for my life. I am talking about a period of four months and 20 days, a lifetime crammed into a few months, totally unplanned and unpremeditated. In the words of the poet Verlaine from 'Chanson d'Automne':

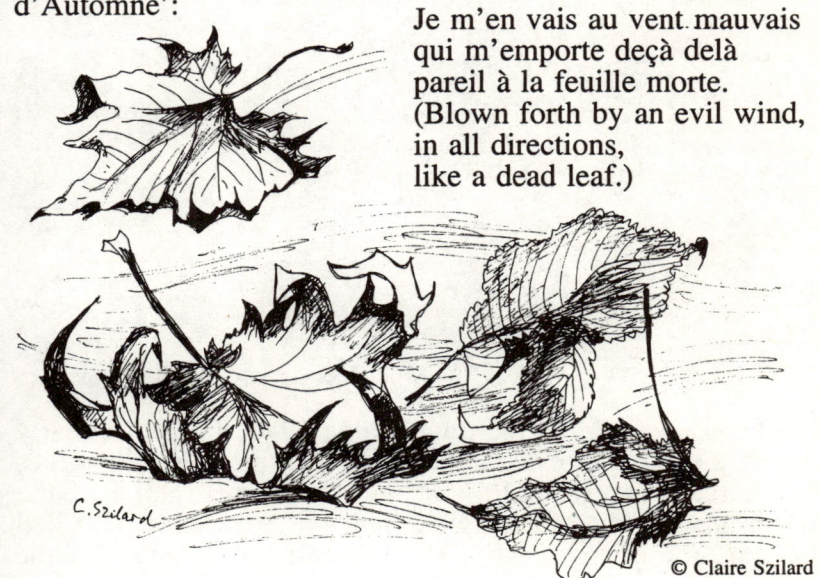

> Je m'en vais au vent mauvais
> qui m'emporte deçà delà
> pareil à la feuille morte.
> (Blown forth by an evil wind,
> in all directions,
> like a dead leaf.)

© Claire Szilard

But we were safe at the end of the journey and my life had taken a new and different turn.

Some incidents and circumstances leading up to the crisis I have already referred to. I shall endeavour here to give a clear, crisp, chronological account of happenings based on my cryptic notes written in French, in minute purple handwriting, on scraps of paper. In June 1940 I was a month short of 15 years of age.

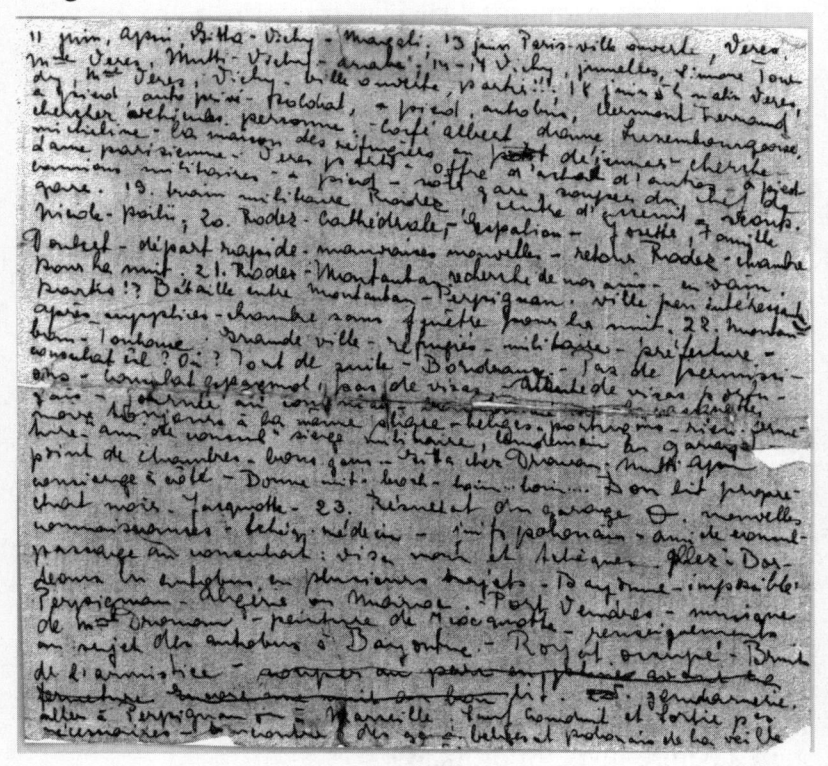

The scene is Paris, the month June 1940, a beautiful early summer having followed a magnificent spring. German armies had already overrun Holland and Belgium in spite of the agreements of the Munich Conference of September 1938 and all the promises of peace. The indomitable defences of the

Maginot line had holes and the German forces penetrated with ease as though it were a perforated cardboard wall and were pouring into northern France. I remember hearing thuds of gunfire in my Paris home, coming ever closer. I shall not forget the procession of carts and anything on wheels, laden with people, mattresses, bundles, bird cages, trundling down the Boulevard Magenta, Paris, at the top of our road (Rue des Petits Hôtels).

History is repeating itself and we have seen again similar scenes in the lands that were once Yugoslavia.

The time had come for us to leave. The dangers were obvious and imminent. But we were foreigners in a foreign land, Czechoslovak citizens in France. Every week we had to report to the 'Préfécture' (police station) for yet another stamp in our residence permit. More papers and permits were required to come and go and above all to leave Paris. My parents filled in the required application forms for an exit permit and we had to wait for this piece of paper before departure was authorised. There must have been thousands of applications and chaos reigned. It so happened that my Father's and my permit surfaced in the sea of red tape but my Mother's application got lost. I think it was for my sake that my parents took the heart-rending decision for the two of us, Father and me, to leave and for my Mother to stay behind and follow as soon as possible. Trains were still running and the destination was to be Vichy, the heart and centre of France, where we had lived before in the winter of 1939. The meeting place and rendezvous was to be our old address, Villa Magali, Rue Mounin. But now it was a different Vichy, a wartime town with troops either preparing for battle or escape and throngs of refugees from the north pouring in. The following text is an almost verbatim transcript and translation of my notes, started before my 15th birthday.

11 June 1940: Paris

French President Paul Reynaud's speech – a last call for help to the USA, occupation of Paris suburbs – partial defeat of France. Apu, Gitta left Paris by train for Vichy, Villa Magali.

13 June 1940: Vichy

Paris was declared 'open city' – no fighting within the city but undisturbed passage for German armies. Still no signs of Mutti in Vichy. With bated breath Apu listened to the radio news in our small boarding house bedroom, news of advancing armies and total chaos. We had given up hope of ever finding Mutti again. Apu was totally desolate and distressed. Then, in the early hours of the morning, perhaps 3 o'clock of June 14th, gentle footsteps down the corridor, a little tap on the door, and there she was! The joy of being together, and we were never separated again during our flight. She told her story: Madame Doulcet's sister Madame Depoit (from 7 Rue des Petits Hôtels) accompanied her to the station (Gare de Lyon) and led her through a sea of desperate humanity waiting and thronging onto trains. By then permits were irrelevant – and of course Mutti hadn't got hers. In the teeming crowd Madame Depoit found an Arab gentleman, who was better than Mutti at elbowing his way through crowds and he led her, I shall never know how or why, towards the train up the steps into a crowded carriage, and it was said to be the last train leaving Paris for Vichy before the total collapse of France. [In my thoughts I have always blessed this nameless Arab who saved my Mother!]

14–17 June 1940: Vichy

Relatively peaceful happy days! I met again my school friends, the twins Madeleine and Yvonne Stouff from Belfort who were still there, waiting for their parents. Mr and Mrs Büchler, refugees, who were still living in what seemed decadent splendour. The chestnut trees lining the wide park lanes by the spa pump house were lush and enormous. Late in the evening of June 17th, the news came through that Vichy was declared 'open city'.

18 June 1940: Vichy

We left at 5 in the morning, on foot, carrying a small case each, direction south, Apu, Mutti and I, Mr and Mrs Veres... A private car stopped and gave us a short lift. We continued on foot and met a French soldier. He had thrown away his weapons like so many others, he was dirty and unshaven, walking south with us. A bus turned up from nowhere, we all got on and arrived in Clermont Ferrand. We went to Café Albert in the centre, a crowded café for light refreshments. There was a lady from Luxembourg called Micheline, another still well-dressed lady from Paris and many others talking and discussing the news. We were directed to a refugee centre for breakfast and were offered a car as a gift which we did not accept. Bread was already confiscated for the advancing German armies, we were advised to leave as quickly as possible. We started out on foot, it was hot, dusty and there was machine-gun fire to be heard. We had occasional lifts in military vehicles, continued on foot and were finally welcomed by the station master at Cahors. He offered us food and a bed.

19 June 1940: Cahors

We got on a military train and arrived at Rodez. The scout centre was open for us and many other refugees.

20 June 1940: Rodez

I can't remember how we got to Montauban. Even on the run Apu found things and places of interest. So *en route* we went to the beautiful red brick cathedral. From Montauban we made our way to Espalion, the residence of Madame Doulcet and her daughter Josette, our benefactors. I think my parents hoped to stay there a while. But the news was bad, dangers imminent; we left suddenly and returned quickly to Rodez where we found a room for the night.

21 June 1940: Rodez

The next port of call was again Montauban, a hot, dusty, uninteresting city. We looked for family Veres, but in vain. Perhaps they had already left. After much pleading we found a room without a window for the night.

22 June 1940: Montauban

We arrived in Toulouse mid-morning. It seemed a large, busy city teeming with activity, full of soldiers, military craft and so many refugees. Surely there would be a 'Préfécture' and a Czechoslovak embassy. We needed papers and permits and help in order to proceed. We needed permission to go west to Bordeaux, where we might take a boat to New York. Permission was refused absolutely.

We waited for ages at the Spanish embassy, but they would not grant any more visas that day. The 'mairie' (town hall) where there was an endless queue of hopefuls, Belgians, French, Poles, Czechs: nothing doing. The Portuguese embassy was closed but a cellar window was ajar; the caretaker claimed to be the Consul's friend and promised hope for the following day. That night a total stranger, Madame Drouaut, whose house was next to the Portuguese embassy, offered to look after me; the caretaker of the adjoining house offered shelter for Mutti and Apu: ['*Une bonne nuit au bon lit propre, les Boches loin, loin*' (a peaceful night in a good clean bed, the Huns far, far away) was the staccato diary entry for that evening]. Madame Drouaut had a black cat and an artist daughter called Jacquotte whose bright paintings were on the walls of my bedroom.

23 June 1940: Toulouse

The nearby garage was to be the unofficial meeting place for refugees, the gathering place for the exchange of news, advice, rumours. There was a Polish Jew and another Czech Doctor and behold! The Portuguese

Consul's friend from the previous day! We followed him back to the Portuguese embassy, he went inside, we waited endlessly, a queue formed, the underground window opened again and the drill was as follows: present passports together with banknote through the window with vertical bars, after a few moments, out came the passport without francs but a piece of paper with the text in Portuguese which was to be copied. (Apu wrote the visa text in his own handwriting into our three passports.) The passports with text and banknotes went back through the window with railings; a few moments later they were pushed out again, complete with official stamps and signatures. We became proud owners of a Portuguese visa of questionable legality. [At that point in our travels, we collected papers, permits and clung at straws. Portugal, a country not at war, became a pipe-dream out of the blue.] We bumped again into the Czech Doctor, you always met up with old acquaintances. He was full of advice and information: why don't we take the bus to Bordeaux in several stages as there wouldn't be a direct one!

Bayonne, south of Bordeaux was no longer possible (I didn't know why). Alternatively, go to Perpignan and then via Port Vendres towards Spain and make either for Algeria or Morocco. [The world was our oyster. I felt all excited.]

We enquired about times of buses. I heard the dreadful news; Royan, north of Bordeaux, occupied by the Germans. There were rumours of an armistice. What does that mean? Now there was so much chaos and panic the police no longer issued exit papers or '*sauf-conduit*'. One no longer cared.

We had picnic supper in the city centre park, in pouring rain, before the gates were locked. Back once more to Madame Drouaut's house and my comfortable bed. She would have offered hospitality forever.

24 June 1940: Toulouse

We bought bus tickets for Perpignan, got ready and set out after a picnic in front of St Jean Cathedral. That night we got as far as Carcassonne, together with thousands like ourselves and spent the night in the clammy foyer of a hotel, dozing. There was gunfire in the distance.

25 June 1940: Carcassonne

The journey by rickety bus and on foot continued through Narbonne to Perpignan. A 'Mistral' was blowing hard. [Later I found out that the local wind, the charmer of the region, the wind blowing the clouds away, is really called Tramontane.] We found accommodation at the local Girls' College – Collège de Jeunes Filles. Apu as well. A busy day followed: a visit to a crowded office to obtain the Moroccan visa at the Spanish embassy.

26 June 1940: Perpignan

More official business: on to the Spanish Embassy for the promised Spanish visa, cost 11 francs. All seemed to go smoothly with the help of bribes; packets of cigarettes slid in all directions. Bureau Central Militaire de la Circulation.

27 June 1940: Perpignan

We said 'Goodbye and many thanks' to the nuns of the Girls' College, took a bus, exit south, direction Spain. There was much talk, rumours, excitement on the bus. We were talking to a lovely Spanish lady in a bright red blouse, a young girl Hélène and her parents. Someone whispered: 'the frontier is closed'. Indeed we found on arrival that the frontier between France and Spain at the township of Le Perthus was closed until further notice.

28 June–9 July 1940: Le Perthus

We settled down to life in Le Perthus, waiting for the frontier to open, waiting, waiting, and there were hundreds of others. Facing Spain, the right side of the high street of Le Perthus was French, the left side Spanish, followed by an area that was 'No Man's Land'. The official frontier post was situated a few yards out of the village. [The layout of the main street has not changed.] My parents found a small room for the three of us in the local French grocer's shop above, chez Marianne, a little friendly Catalan lady, always dressed in black. Every morning, at about 9 o'clock, we left, carrying our picnic bag, personal papers and a small rug, called at the local bakery to buy a loaf of crunchy freshly baked bread, and at the food shop on the high street for a tin of sardines and a kilogram of sweet, large, shapeless tomatoes, occasionally a packet of biscuits, and proceeded to the frontier.

There was a grassy embankment in the heart of the mountains (Pyrénées) with some shade from the odd shrub. France lay behind and Spain, the promised land, a few yards before us. There we stayed with all the waiting hopefuls until night-time, about 7 o'clock, when the frontier would close officially. With us were numerous bored but very friendly Spanish frontier police, now out of work. After 7 we could walk back to Marianne's house. Every night she prepared a beef broth with vegetables in a black '*marmite*' (crock pot) on her open kitchen range – the aroma would greet us as the door opened. '*La soupe est ce qu'il y a de mieux quand l'estomac est fatigué*' (there is nothing like soup when your stomach is off) she said every evening as she ladled the broth into our plates. The little room upstairs was cool and comfortable. At night I could hear footsteps and Franco-Spanish words from downstairs until very late. It was a veritable smugglers' den – so I thought. Mutti dried our washed handkerchiefs on the dressing table mirror so that they should have the cared for, ironed look. Each day, from the 28th of June until the 8th July, had exactly the same pattern and routine. But there was always excitement, interest, talk and anticipation at our frontier post!

There were Spanish customs officers in their sage green uniforms and peaked caps, smart, smiling, all too keen to teach Spanish, to accept cigarettes, chat and laugh. There was luscious Carmen who tried to attract the attentions of a French officer, and obese Monsieur Le Maire (lord mayor) from I don't know which French township, complete with his pretty secretary. We met Henri, a Flemish Belgian and his family with whom we were to share a car and travel further; Paskusz, a tall central European with a handlebar moustache; a lady in black, taciturn, covered in diamonds. A huge Belgian family, complete with family pets; a chemist, a fruiterer, a British Consul and a Dutch Baroness. There was a mysterious Hungarian, another person of unknown or undisclosed nationality, a professional black-marketeer who still dealt openly in everything, and I was aware of a flow of pesetas and French francs. There was a stuck-up horrible Polish lady, a group of lugubrious men who seemed like the Gestapo, a very proud lady whose silk stockings were too big for her, a small rotund dark-looking director. Now and again one of the phones rang and some exceptions were made: a small group of French people and an Anglo-American couple were allowed to pass into Spain.

There were a few dogs hopping about, Titi and Alexi, and white goats who had no frontier restrictions. We met a Czech diplomat from Munkačevo, Paskusz and a few other handlebar moustaches! Yolande was big and friendly and produced potatoes for us from nowhere. One day we braved the forest and had a communal feast and walk and the Spanish officers whom we met smiled, joined us for picnic lunch and didn't shoot.

8 July 1940: Le Perthus

Official news came through that the frontier would be opened the following day. [The stamp in my passport for 8 July confirms exit from France, Le Perthus and '*entrada*', entry into Spain at La Jonquera. Passport evidence is there forever: '27 June, arrival in Perthus; 2 July, Frontier closed, Spanish visa extended'.]

Arrangements were made for Mutti, Apu and myself to travel to Morocco by car with Belgian Henri, wife and sick child, Miriam, free of charge because Apu was acting as 'travelling doctor'. How Henri managed to have car, petrol and money I shall never know.

Henri the driver and Apu were in front, Madame, Mutti, the sick little girl and I squashed in the back. It was hot, clammy, sticky and tight but we were on the move again!

9 July 1940: between Le Perthus and La Jonquera

So we were off, the three of us and Henri and family, crammed in their 'Old type Ford'. In his Yiddish German accent Henri repeated many times the story of his luxurious 15-roomed apartment and 14 suits hanging in his wardrobe in Brussels, all left behind. Miriam's chamber pot was smelly and clonking as we drove along. The route was through Figueras to Barcelona where we stayed one night in the lap of luxury, at Hotel Tomes, Plaza Cataluña, category B, paid for in francs and pesetas. It all seemed like a holiday again and we all went on a boat ride in the port.

11 July 1940: Barcelona

We drove north-west, over the mountains, through Montserrat. On the hills we feasted on stolen almonds, otherwise tins, tins, more tins. There were castles, forts, ruins perched on rock. The town of Tarrega was in ruins from bombardments in the recent civil war. On and on through hills, olive groves to Zaragoza, 'the town of a hundred towers' where we stayed the night, having found a room with much difficulty.

12 July 1940: Zaragoza

A dead town, the only inhabitants seemed to be cats and dogs. On, on, over endless flat mountain formations and barren desert land towards Calatayud where we stopped for what I regarded as 'a lovely meal', from there through Guadalajara and a night stop at Alcala. We were now in the land of Don Quixote and the windmills of Cervantes, Apu's favourite author. Again, it was hard to find a room for the night. Alcala was a bustling town, full of soldiers and energetic throngs of people. I drank goat's milk for the first time.

13 July 1940: Madrid

We left for Madrid and bumped into Betty who had been at Le Perthus with us, and we had difficulty finding a room: finally it was Hotel M, in Calle José Antonio, one of several hotels within the same building. There were hollow buildings all around us, craters, perforated façades and rubble. I was struck by the large number of blind and hobbling people injured during the recent civil war.

14, 15 and 16 July 1940: Madrid

I well remember the first night at Hotel M, *'chasse aux punaises'* or 'hunting bed lice'. In the early hours of the morning, during an uncomfortable, hot night, bedroom doors were creaking and gently opening and characters in gaudy pyjamas or kimono-type dressing gowns drifted into the corridor, scratching, waving arms, beating at black things. Yes, we were attacked by a gigantic army of persistent bedbugs and it was more comfortable out of bed than amongst the sheets. I don't know how we coped on the two subsequent nights.

In the daytime we combed Madrid in search of embassies. The British embassy was situated opposite the heavily armed and guarded German embassy. I was terribly frightened.

We were well received at the British embassy and as the passport entry shows, we were granted a visa for the UK: 'Accompanies her father, confirmed by telegram'. Signed by the Assistant Consul: Gratis.

Whether the British visa was vital for coming to Britain or not, I shall never know. The long and short of it, we now had official permission to go to paradise, although the sequence was not at all clear. We were travelling *en route* to what was then French Morocco.

I shall never forget the Prado and the impression El Greco's paintings had made on me. I have seen many more El Grecos since and visited the Prado again, but the colours and shapes have never again seemed so strong or vivid.

We left Madrid and travelled at night, to save money and to be spared daytime heat.

17 July 1940: on the road, having left Madrid

More desolate country, 'desert, desert, desert' through royal Aranjuez, then Manzanares and a meal stop at La Carolina, then Linares, finally Montoro for the night. The men couldn't decide on the route: was it to be by Sevilla, Granada or Malaga?

18 July 1940: Montoro

We drove through Cordoba and Sevilla, stopping briefly in both, then at Puerto de Santa Maria for the night. First glimpse of the Atlantic Ocean. A scruffy hotel with unpleasantness all the way, problems with garaging the car.

19 July 1940: Puerto de Santa Maria

More problems with petrol, dollars, hotel bills; we were

overcharged. We followed the route to Cadiz, where the Mediterranean meets the Atlantic Ocean, from there to Tarifa and finally to Algeciras, with no time to lose: for the sea crossing to Africa we got tickets and drove onto the small boat for Ceuta, Spanish Morocco, North Africa. The boat was crowded with families of African women and children, the sea in the Straits of Gibraltar was very choppy. You could see the rock of Gibraltar in the distance, the outline of Africa with the Atlas mountains before us: indeed, a new continent. On arrival in the early evening, the heat was even more intense. Dry, scorching African heat and a sea of humanity: the white of women's clothing and a mass of bright red dots, the 'fez' or 'caps' worn by men. There was absolute chaos. Young boys aggressively offered their wares as well as hotel addresses. I was very frightened and felt threatened. Petrol was cheap but our car broke down. I don't know how we got to Tetouan, Spanish Morocco, nor to our hotel that night. Also, there were disagreements with the hotel owner. Apu lodged complaints and we went to court where a theatrical judge officiated with the help of an Arab interpreter. We won the case and were refunded some money!

21 July 1940: Tetouan, Spanish Morocco

We left at 5 o'clock in the morning, perhaps to avoid the intense heat. We drove through Souk-el-Arba, Sorache, Alcazarquivir, Loco... A different world! We saw the first camels and African donkeys or mules and endless stretches of sandy soil. In an Arab café we met a nice Frenchman who was full of information. We ate white, round flat Spanish bread and had a long discussion about the Arab way of life. We were now due to cross into French Morocco and drove through the first French Moroccan villages, so very different from Spanish Morocco, a more European Africa. I fell ill, the very first time since leaving Paris. I had high fever. '*Gitta* malade;

fièvre...' We were making for Rabat, the administrative capital of French Morocco.

22 July 1940: Rabat, French Morocco, Hotel Orsay

We said goodbye to our companions, Henri and family, and went our separate ways. Rabat was a beautiful luxurious southern city, palm lined with lush vegetation and luxurious buildings and wide boulevards.

Georges Gayet, Lili and family were the real reason for calling at Rabat. We were to make contact with Georges, my father's Hungarian cousin Lili's husband, a French general very highly placed in the hierarchy. It was Georges whom my father visited in Paris before the occupation of Czechoslovakia for discussions (and he subsequently stayed on and never returned). This time also high hopes were pinned 'on the family', on their help and advice at that difficult moment in our lives. We found the grand family house in 44 Rue de L'Oeuvre, Rabat, only to discover that Georges and Lili were out and their four children, my second cousins, were being looked after by a governess. My memories are hazy, but I never saw Georges, only Lili and the children on the following day.

Reception was totally frigid and we were not even asked in. So we found a room at 'Hôtel de France' that night and my parents were very disappointed. From the hotel room window I could see a harem, an enclosed garden where the Muslim ladies were comporting themselves like in a film! We went to my first Moroccan market, then on to Casablanca. [I do not remember how we travelled.]

23 July–14 September 1940: Casablanca

We are at last in Casablanca, our final destination, end of our journey (or so we believed). Our hotel was called 'Ali Baba', situated somewhere near the centre. We didn't stay long.

At the hotel, we were plagued by large, flying cockroaches and other worries. The Café de France in Casablanca, by the main post office, was the focal point for all refugees; it did not take long to find out everything. There we heard that several central European families resident in Casablanca were offering hospitality for the homeless, for the likes of us.

We were invited to spend our Casablanca days with ex-Hungarian family, the Földes: mother, father, little boy and girl, in 7 rue des Hirondelles, a residential district of Casablanca.

Until that moment in time the three of us were independent, free and 'on the move'. Rue des Hirondelles for me was a huge anticlimax, restrictive, inhibiting and sad. I learned to understand the meaning of the word 'charity' and the difficulties of having to be grateful. I disliked Monsieur and Madame Földes, both children were horrible and they took it out of me whenever they could. There were no more objectives, nothing to look forward to, and my parents were visibly subdued. I read everything I could lay my hands on, and was duly labelled 'bluestocking'. The meals were dull and formal and I had to be helpful but didn't know how. There were, however, a few highlights. I managed to push a bathing costume into my tiny hand case in Paris: that meant I could occasionally go to the beach and enjoy the Atlantic waves. The Arab and Jewish markets, Mecca and Medina, in the heart of Casablanca, were colourful, noisy and fascinating and I could have spent my days there. I was bought a pair of leather sandals and navy blue baggy Moroccan silk pyjamas. During our regular visits to the post office and Café de France, we met many old and made many new friends. Refugee gossip and animated discussions had become part of my life. I loved to listen. We met and talked with Roger, Fassenak, Palituksi, Bénuska, Zsófika, Almed, Thursch, Pinto, Cohen, Marie Rosenberg, Moische and others. Then there was Faludy György, and his wife Wally. They were different, less downcast, not new arrivals. Faludy was a beautiful sunburnt man, with wild dark eyes and a mop of hair. I was told that he had donned Arab clothes and gone on a camel trek to the Sahara Desert with Nomads; I was impressed. Wally, his wife, was young, beautiful and she gave me a white summer skirt, embroidered in red.

Faludy is still a Hungarian poet of some reputation, and I am a great admirer of his early work; it makes it so much more personal to have known him. I have followed his career since. I treasure his translation and adaptation of François Villon's *Testament*, other poems and his autobiography, *My Life in Hell*.

My 15th birthday, on the 30th July was a non-event, I can't recollect anything about it. Apu must have been doing some medical work during our stay in Casablanca to pass the time and earn some money. I remember seeing fans made of palm leaves for the sick.

Towards the end of August, less than four weeks after our arrival, there were more rumours and news of uncertainty and danger: French Morocco was a French possession, and as a result of the defeat of France, it automatically came under the jurisdiction of Pétain's Vichy France, indirectly a German sphere of influence. All speculations came to a head when Georges Gayet sent an urgent message to my Father, telling him that French Morocco was no longer safe for us and to plan an exit route as quickly as possible. No doubt through his intervention, we obtained telephone permission for exit papers, issued on 30 August 1940, to leave Morocco, destination Portugal, on the move, to escape yet again. Passport entry on departure read 'Extension – new transit visa for Portugal, final destination England'.

Georges had taken our safety seriously. I contacted his son, my second cousin, many years later in Paris but there was no further contact.

So we were back again to planning, investigating, manipulating. They had talked about a fishing barge to Tangier on the 10th September, also about another vessel appropriately called 'Ange et Diable' (angel and devil), to some unknown destination, and about many other possibilities, amongst others 'Mar Azul' (Blue Sea), a 150 or 80 ton vessel, due to leave Casablanca for Lisbon on September 14th. Mar Azul it was to be, and we bought a straw mattress each and enough tins of sardines to last the journey, and most important, boat tickets at a considerable price. I can't remember any farewells. I think I was glad to leave.

14 September 1940: Casablanca, on Mar Azul

Embarkation was at 10 o'clock in the morning and many people crowded onto the boat with their case and mattresses, but departure was only after 5 o'clock in the afternoon, after the 'Consul du Port' or Harbour Master had checked all our papers and countersigned the list of travellers. As soon as we had left harbour, nearly all were seasick; there was black tar everywhere trodden into everything and a storm was brewing and the sea was raging all night. We were spread out on mattresses like sardines, according to family groups, in the 'Calle' or hold, where the cargo would normally be placed. This was our home, except for brief trips to the top deck where the only toilet was situated. There we cooked, ate, slept, talked, felt uncomfortable and nauseated. I can still see a wooden ladder leading to top deck where nimble sailors in royal blue overalls would climb up and down like monkeys, carrying full or empty enamel chambers duly tipped overboard into the Atlantic. We soon got to know Csacske, a Spanish lady, family Kochmann, Klein, Holas, Šedivka, Otakar and Mana Kraus, Klapholz, Uzel, Friemann, Pollak, most of them from Czechoslovakia, people wanting to go to England to join the forces and help in the war effort. Amongst them were musicians and they led the nightly sing-song of Czechoslovak folk music.

15 September 1940: Mar Azul at sea

The Atlantic Ocean lapping, the Bay of Biscay at its worst, the sea getting wilder and wilder. Everyone sick, except for little children, Apu and Holas, a Czech writer. I remember sleeping uneasily to the sound of creaking wood, lashing waves and seasick fellow travellers.

16 September 1940: Mar Azul

Another bad night of rough seas. In the distance at last the coastline of Portugal becoming visible, although the sea was still raging and rocking the vessel. Late evening the Bay of Lisbon appears on the horizon and we now brave the wooden ladder to top deck in order to see land!

17 September 1940: Lisbon Harbour, Mar Azul

We wash and tidy as best as we can, all 250 or so travellers. The sun has risen and what a splendid view of Lisbon, our destination! Mar Azul throws anchor some distance from the quay side. 'Service de Santé portugaise', Portuguese Sanitary Officers, arrive by launch to check I don't know what. We can see a large British boat with Tommies, naval ratings in full uniform on board. Also there, floating in all its splendour, was the original sailing boat in which Vasco de Gama, the explorer, sailed the Indian Ocean and returned to Portugal in September 1499. Hours go by. Towards evening the Captain makes an announcement: all French and British for landing, please; not the rest of us, we were not included. A basket of food and fruit appears from nowhere, again not for us, like to Tantalus who could not reach his food and drink in the Underworld. The hours go by, another night on Mar Azul!

18 September 1940: Lisbon Harbour, Mar Azul

A whole day of waiting. We are now familiar with numerous vessels all around us floating on the tide. It is all unreal, we can't understand... Then, at 10 o'clock at night – all off! We are herded into a Black Maria – Portuguese police van – 'voiture des criminels' – and are taken to the prison of Caxias, Reduto di Norte, Forte Caxias near Lisbon, without any explanations. 'Pourquoi?'

19 September 1940–5 October: Caxias

On arrival, we were divided into groups of 'men' and 'women' and allotted separate dormitories of about 30 beds, like a girls' boarding school, I thought. There were 3 meals in the large dining room per day. Breakfast at 8 o'clock consisting of black coffee and brown bread; there was lunch at about 1 o'clock with a bowl of rice and bits of meat which we thought were cat or dog, accompanied by red wine; supper of bread and water. We were seated at long wooden trestle tables and benches. In the afternoons we (only the latest Mar Azul arrivals) were taken out to the grounds or gardens of the fortress where we spent several hours together each day. From the hilltop the view was over the Bay of Lisbon. Aeroplanes and boats were coming and going freely and it was a beautiful sunny late September. Spirits were high, conversation lively and friendships warm. We all had our dormitory stories to tell. In the men's dormitory with Apu was Eduardo and also Antonio, a Portuguese dissident who had been active on the Socialist side in the Spanish civil war, imprisoned indefinitely. He had remained the eternal optimist and cheered the new arrivals with his daily 'good morning' greeting and 'mañana la liberatione' in Spanish [freedom tomorrow].

On the women's side, we knew about our room mate, tall and fair English Miranda, who committed the crime of wearing a bikini on a Portuguese beach before her imprisonment; Dutch Marijke, a lovely young woman in her early twenties, who had an illegitimate baby, perhaps by a Portuguese man. Mutti arranged for barter with the thin, shrivelled, small dormitory cleaning lady: she swapped Apu's daily ration of wine for milk because of his stomach ulcers. The exchange took place secretly in the dormitory after the maid would call huskily 'Señora, leche' (in Portuguese) (my lady, milk). There were other rather uncommunicative and uncouth women, 'Les personnes mal élevées dans notre chambre'. One Sunday, visitors came to Caxias prison grounds to 'see' the refugees. They brought bananas and other goodies and gaped at us. Our witty sarcastic Czech fellow prisoners couldn't take the humiliation of it, to be stared at like animals in a zoo. One of them, probably Uzel, started roaring like a lion, and one by one we all got the message and responded with a concert of animal noises, a cacophony of roars, and proudly refused the morsels thrown to us. I don't know what the benefactors thought: I would have loved a banana but wouldn't dare take one.

With hindsight maybe our reaction was ungracious and we were embittered by circumstances but to me, age 15, it all seemed a big laugh!

I mentioned earlier that our fellow prisoners were people of some consequence. At that time in history it took great courage and foresight to abandon everything in central Europe and face the unknown; it was not yet a mass evacuation or exodus. The Holocaust had not begun. Therefore the company present consisted mostly of witty professional people, writers, poets, musicians, journalists, politicians ahead of events. It so happened that Šedivka was a violinist member of a quartet, Otakar Kraus an opera singer and other personalities.

We were not ill treated but humiliated and we were not free. I don't know anything about our official status at Caxias or the real attitude of the prison management. Let it be said that at that time Portugal was a neutral country, trying to remain that way, traumatically torn between the warring parties, Britain and Germany, and governed by Sanlazaar, a reactionary autocrat with the presence of his German trained secret police. For Germany's sake we, the Mar Azul contingent, had to be stopped. For the sake of Portugal's historic allegiance with Great Britain, the will of Britain could not be overridden or ignored. To our knowledge, no one other than the secret police and prison authorities knew of our existence and plight.

During our stay in Caxias we were granted one privilege: a weekly visit by prison van to Lisbon centre to a café on the central Plaza Mayor. We were accompanied by polite, unassuming prison officers and could spend a few hours drinking coffee or lemonade, be part of ordinary life and feel almost free.

On the occasion of our third Lisbon café visit, a letter had been written, I don't know by whom, containing facts about our circumstances, duly signed by everyone and addressed to the British Embassy, Lisbon. One of the officers had been bribed or cajoled into posting the letter, though I never found out any details. The result was electric and dramatic: the following morning, 5 October, after a brief telephone call from the British Embassy to Caxias Prison, we were to be released immediately. In style, by 'Black Maria', we were driven to the port of Lisbon, then led onto the moored vessel HMS *Neuralia*, and henceforth on British territory and under British jurisdiction. We three were given a cabin, first class, sparkling and with crisp sheets. The gong called us all to supper: tables lavishly set out with starched white table linen, gleaming silver cutlery, Indian waiters in colourful suits and head-dress waiting on us during what seemed to be an endless meal. Someone started to giggle, we all broke out into helpless laughter – the contrast, the idiosyncrasy of it all after Caxias just proved to be too much!

6 October 1940: HMS Neuralia, *Lisbon Harbour*

Chaotic search for luggage. Between us we probably had very little and this might have surprised the crew. After loud hooting, HMS *Neuralia* sailed out of harbour, and in the distance, on the cliff, we could see Caxias!

A series of large, long English meals! I was surprised – if not put off – to be offered grilled kippers for breakfast. The sea was calm – and we were now gliding along on a 9,000 ton vessel, a far cry from rickety Mar Azul.

Towards evening we sighted the coast of Atlantic Spain but where were we going? 'Quelle direction?'

7 October 1940: HMS Neuralia, *at sea*

A noisy night! Gunfire and wartime fireworks in all directions. Lots of black smoke in the Straits of Gibraltar, the rock of Gibraltar on one side and North Africa facing us once again.

8 October 1940: HMS Neuralia

Slowly heading towards the Rock and landing at Gibraltar. Disembarkation at midday. My parents and I, also a few of the original party, were given rooms at Hotel Wintergarden in Gibraltar, a hotel now empty of tourists but filled with soldiers, sailors and refugees.

I can't remember anything about daily life in Gibraltar; my diary notes say nothing. It all seemed like a luxurious holiday in the beautiful autumn sunshine surrounded by subtropical vegetation. All civilians had been evacuated and those humans remaining were mostly sailors. There was also a considerable population of monkeys, not in the slightest bit put off by humans. On 17 October after a timeless stay in Lotusland we were informed that departure would be the following day.

Back to the Port of Gibraltar, and our boat was to be HMS *Reina del Pacifico*, a magnificent, imposing vessel. We were given first-class cabins because Apu was a doctor and his services might be needed. After embarkation in the course of the morning, we finally steamed out in the evening, destination unknown.

19 October 1940: HMS Reina del Pacifico

After embarkation we were all called on deck to muster station for safety drill with lifeboats. This happened several times a day but no actual emergency arose. Life on board was comfortable, we had grown accustomed again to a cosy way of life. But there was much excitement: the Battle of Britain was in full swing, the seas were mined and there were naval attacks and counter-attacks, shelling, smoke and noise. On October 21st we heard about a night-time battle against two torpedo boats and we were always concerned and worried. We were far out at sea, no land visible and much speculation as to destination. Rumours had it – and there was always news circulating – that we were heading for Canada. At one point it felt like a 360° turn, whether it was a military manoeuvre or change of destination, I shall never know. [My notes peter out, most of the rest is just memory or record.] The night before landing I had a dream. I had started English lessons briefly in school in Paris and English language lessons were now filling a few hours on the *Reina del Pacifico*. My dream was spoken in English, it was technicolour about England.

24 October 1940: HMS Reina del Pacifico

I had a dream...

A polite teaparty in a conventional English parlour. A long oak table newly set for afternoon tea. Tall, upright, white-haired ladies with false teeth were pouring tea out of silver teapots and passing plates of thinly cut bread and butter and there were pots and pots of marmalade. The conversation flowed: phrases from my school textbook.

According to record books from the Greenwich Maritime Museum, HMS *Reina del Pacifico* docked in Liverpool on 25 October 1940. That is when we must have arrived.

There are no more scraps of paper with tiny purple writing,

but I remember the rest. We remained in quarantine for health and other checks until cleared. Then, by night train, I think probably on 28 October, we were taken from Liverpool to London. The train stopped several times because of a ferocious air battle. It was the height of the Blitz, and the Battle of Britain, and bombs were falling and exploding in all directions. Anti-aircraft guns were in full force. It was a dramatic irony that we arrived at the detention centre in Norwood, near Croydon, on 29 October 1940, exactly one year after reaching France from Czechoslovakia, full of hope for our new life there which was not to be.

From Norwood, cynically referred to by fellow travellers as 'purgatory', those of us who were found to be 'in order' by our government in exile and other organisations were given an address, a key, a ration book, an identity card and a National Assistance Book and we departed to our new allotted home.

In our case it was Hackney, journey's end, and from there my life in Britain unfolded.

This is also a convenient stopping place for my story. I can still remember the first 14 years and the horrendous fifteenth year of my life with utmost clarity and affection. Those years of change, contrast, danger, excitement and history are my special personal treasures and the subject of this book. I was a mere uprooted shoot in the course of world chaos, but the cutting has taken root again and I have survived. I have been spared the Holocaust. My story has taught me to love life.

The subsequent 58 years, my life in Britain, my home, have been full, rich and sad, with highlights and memories and they merge into one another. But they are private and my own. They are not part of this story.

EPILOGUE

Budapest, December 1997

Anny is dead, my cousin and closest relative. I am now the last of that generation. She always talked of dying, ever since I can remember. Her health was frail, her thoughts were in the past and about the day she would die, all alone. That is why I was convinced that she was immortal and the news of her death came as a great shock.

We had just spent two weeks together in southern Hungary, at Gyula, close to Szeged, where our fathers were born. She loved that land and put off her operation, postponed the dreaded moment, so as to spend time together in October 1997, the autumn of her life. She was unusually serene and jolly, like Cyrano de Bergerac in the Convent Garden before his death. The last morning in Budapest, before our departure and return to England, she seemed carefree and elated, quite out of character.

She died one day later. The circumstances of her death were wrought with suspicion and mystery. She died alone, and was found about three days later, her nails rose-pink, beautifully manicured on the morning of her death, the rest pitiful. She had been spared the operation.

Her funeral, or rather cremation ceremony, took place one month later, on a cold, bleak December afternoon, at Farkasrét (Wolves' Meadow) cemetery, a bus ride away from her Budapest home. The occasion was beautiful, dignified and wholly abiding by her wishes. The actual cremation had to be carried out at an earlier unspecified time and her ashes placed in a personally selected casket, bedecked in flowers. We gathered in a splendid, discreetly and tastefully decorated hall, in a semicircle, around the casket which was placed on a stretcher-like table. Lesley, my eldest daughter from England, Michael, my son from Texas, and I were the chief mourners, dressed in deep black as directed. We were due to receive all arriving guests, distant family, friends, ex-colleagues, journalists, trade union members. Tears flowed freely, embraces were overpowering, eulogies ran high, and we three from a distant island, close to Anny, felt somewhat overpowered and confused. Who were all these small, rotund people in hats, who had rarely come near Anny in her lifetime, and who were now so heartbroken?

Our chosen music to precede the ceremony was Mozart's *Requiem*, on cassette, because no other audio equipment was available. The cassette machine was antiquated and the sounds were groaning, grating, squeaking. Then followed the speeches: the official address by the director of the crematorium, duly briefed by the knowledgeable about Anny's CV, beautifully spoken, accompanied by extracts from poetry. He was a distant gentleman, uncommunicative and would not part with the script of his speech. Then followed a young friend, Borika, a lovely, sorrowful academic who waxed sentimentally and whose connections with Anny we never found out. Finally, my daughter Lesley read a brief English poem by W.H. Auden, expressive and to the point.

The casket and stretcher were then placed onto a hearse, and the starter-motor roaring, the limousine began to speed along at 3 kilometres per hour, we three chief mourners in deep black, my children either side of me, immediately behind the limousine, inhaling black clouds of exhaust fumes, the rest of the congregation bearing flowers, in disorderly formation, chatting softly and following.

The path was slightly uphill, past graves and memorial stones and statues, trees and flowers either side of us, until we reached the final destination.

The casket was to be placed by the bearers onto the stone ledge or 'cubbyhole' of a unit housing five other places of rest, a 'columbarium', not unlike a solid chest of drawers made of stone, with names engraved onto the front panel. The said gap already housed the casket of Anny's mother, Jankus (Barabás Bélané) and Anny's husband Pista (Dr Berkes István). The marble panel was loose, with Anny's name already engraved, Dr Berkes Istvánné. Most Hungarians remain formal, even in death. A woman usually takes her husband's surname as well as Christian name, as well as title, omitting her own forename. I am sad about this surrender of identity. In life, Anny, Jankus and Pista, existing under one roof in Daróczi út 54, lived in constant discord. Did all three have to remain together in death?

The bearers placed Anny's casket in the gap, by mother and husband, with immediate family flowers, yellow roses on the casket, all other flowers, wreaths and bouquets adorned with wide, inscribed ribbons, on the base. It was left to Michael to give a heartfelt address in English, on behalf of the family, the little ones and our future generations. This was translated by Klári into Hungarian, for the benefit of the congregation.

In a burial, there is earth thrown onto the coffin. Here, after Michael's words, a crematorium mason put the engraved marble front in place, and painstakingly, in complete silence, with trowel in hand and cement, tapping metal against sand, slowly secured the nameplate for ever. Here was the heart-rending finality of the occasion.

We adjourned to the inn opposite, for a pre-arranged meal with freedom of choice, concluded with the traditional cherished family gateau, 'Dobos Torta'. Spirits were good and now relaxed, of like-minded people after a sad occasion. We then dispersed.

On revisiting Anny's place of rest six months later, in a more objective mood, I discovered the monumental graves of musicians Sir George Solti and Bartók, a stone's throw away from Anny. How pleased she would be of their proximity!

I am now returning to the end and the beginning, to the phoenix, the bird which 'rose from the ashes with renewed youth to live through another cycle'. I am referring to the grand but sad clear-out of Anny's home: the rediscovery of her past and also mine; newfound fragments of the story of our ancestors, the tangible and metaphorical memorabilia of a bygone era.

Anny had lived in number 54 for 70 years. Not one letter or calendar had been thrown away. There were bundles of bills, receipts, letters of protest, praise and condolence, love letters, diplomas, membership cards, faded photographs. In drawers we found lisle stockings from the thirties painstakingly darned, dozens of scarves, new and tatty shoes, handbags, pencils and unusable pens or biros; unopened parcels of unused gifts; tins and jars of sugar, rancid flour, stale coffee kept for rainier days; bundles of rags suitable for patching, polishing, mending or refuse collections; books, more books and pictures.

Out of one newspaper parcel from the top shelf in the hall cupboard emerged a suitcase in a felt protective cover: *the suitcase*.

When we were children, in about 1934, Anny and I each received an identical Christmas present from our grandparents in Léva: a small suitcase of embossed calf leather lined in a fine beige fabric, enveloped in a two-tone felt protective cover. I remember how thrilled I was with my present, to receive my very own piece of luggage for all the journeys I longed to make. Indeed, wherever I went after that Christmas, my suitcase came as well.

The case was my hand luggage when we left Bratislava and home in 1939. My case and I arrived in France in the October 1939 and we stayed together. On 11 June 1940, the collapse of France, when we had to flee on foot, with hand luggage only, I carried my little case, although it felt heavy, along the hot, dusty roads of France. In addition to toothbrush and a few clean clothes I had with me a swimsuit and Edmond Rostand's *Cyrano de Bergerac*.

We arrived together in Morocco, in Portugal and finally in England, and the leather no longer had its pristine glow.

Then quieter years followed for the case and me. My family

and I went camping to France in the summer of 1962. Camping material had to be unloaded from the car and tents erected in the dusk of early evening. The following morning we discovered to my horror that the case had gone – it was missing; someone must have found it in the grass and taken it. It was never returned.

Thirty-five years later, whilst clearing out Anny's belongings, there, wrapped in copies of obsolete Hungarian newspapers, from the dusty top shelf of the hall cupboard, emerged gleaming, clean and unused, Anny's suitcase, the double of mine. Here was the lost treasure from Treasure Island, Anny's gift of renewal, memories of our childhood and my beginnings, promises of future voyages, charted or otherwise.

In the words of Archbishop Carey of Canterbury: *'For the sake of our future we must recall the past.'*

FAMILY TREE

My paternal grandparents (1855–1925)
Bruchsteiner, Bernat and Guthard, Janka married, lived in Szeged, southern Hungary, and had five children: a daughter Ilona, and sons Béla, Imre, Gerő and Erwin. Béla, the eldest son, officially changed the family name to Barabás. Erwin Barabás (formerly Bruchsteiner) was my father: Apu (Father) from the Hungarian.

My maternal grandparents (1870–1944) (Omi and Opi to me from the German Granny and Grandad)
Blumenthal, Jónás and Schönstein, Gisela married, lived in Levice (Léva) a town of several political changes and now a part of Slovakia. They had two daughters: Jankus (my aunt) and Rózsi (or Rosalie), my Mother, whom I called Mutti (Mother) from the German. Szilard Janka née Grotte (first cousin to Jankus and Rosalie), mother of Klári (known as Claire Szilard).

Jónás and Gisela (my maternal grandparents) died in Auschwitz concentration camp in April 1944, when they were 74 and 71 years old.

Barabás Béla married Blumenthal Jankus, lived in Budapest, Hungary, and had one daughter, Anny (Anna Maria), who later married Berkes István, and died childless in November 1997.

Béla was deported to Kecskémet, Hungary, in April 1944, and disappeared without trace at the age of 56.

My parents (1896–1976)
Barabás, Erwin, my Father, (Béla's brother), and Blumenthal, Rózsi (Rosalie), (my Mother, and Jankus' sister), married in Bratislava, then Czechoslovakia, and I, Gitta, born in 1925, am their only daughter. Together we fled, travelled and settled in England. My Father died in Stafford in 1961, my Mother in Birmingham in 1976.

I met Robert Ogg at Bangor University. We married in 1948 and had five children. Robert died in 1984.

My children and grandchildren (1950–)
Lesley, married, with three children: Helen, Nicholas and Sarah.
Alison, died in an accident at 21 years of age.
Michael, married, has two daughters: Galen and Maren, and lives in the USA.
Christopher, married, has two daughters: Kathy and Susan.
Penny, married, with three children: Emma, Stephanie and Laurence.

CHRONOLOGY

World events		Family events	
Date	Event	Date	Event
		8 Sept 1896	Erwin born
		9 Dec 1898	Rosalie born
28 July 1914	Murder of Archduke Ferdinand		
July 1914	Outbreak of World War I		
11 Nov 1918	End of World War I	1918	Erwin back from army
28 Oct 1918	Creation of Czechoslovak republic	1918	Erwin takes Czechoslovak citizenship
28 June 1919	Treaty of Versailles	1919	Erwin at University of Prague
June 1919	*Coup d'état* in Hungary	16 Sept 1919	Anny born
		1923	Erwin and Rosalie married and settled in Bratislava
		30 July 1925	Gitta born
		1931	Moved to Konventná 17
1933–1945	Holocaust	1931–1935	German schools

World events		Family events	
Date	Event	Date	Event
Jan 1933	Hitler		
1934	*Kristallnacht*: burning of books		
1935	Nuremberg laws and persecution of Jews	1935–1939	Slovak schools
1934	Assassination of Chancellor Dollfuss		
		1937	Last holiday abroad
11 Mar 1938	*Anschluss* (German occupation of Austria)		
1936–1939	Spanish Civil War		
29 Sept 1938	Congress of Munich (Hitler, Daladier, Mussolini, Chamberlain)		
Sept 1938	One week's mobilisation in Czechoslovakia	23 Sept 1938	Erwin mobilised
Sept 1938	Annexation of Czech territories and creation of Hlinka Slovakia		
15 Mar 1939	Occupation of Prague and Slovakia satellite of Germany	15 Mar 1939	Erwin in Paris and remains

World events		Family events	
Date	Event	Date	Event
1 Sept 1939	Invasion of Poland, outbreak of World War II	12 and 13 Sept 1939	Rosalie and Gitta leave for Budapest and France
		29 Oct 1939	Rosalie and Gitta arrive in Vichy, France
30 Nov 1939	Soviet attack on Finland		
		Jan 1940	Rosalie, Gitta and Erwin move to Paris
April 1940	Himmler establishes Auschwitz, Hitler invades Norway and Denmark		
10 May 1940	Hitler invades Netherlands, Belgium, Luxembourg and N. France		
28 May– 4 June 1940	Dunkirk evacuation		
10 June 1940	Italy declares war		
11 June 1940	Paris declared 'open city'	11 June 1940	Erwin and Gitta leave Paris
		12 June 1940	Rosalie leaves Paris, last train

World events		Family events	
Date	Event	Date	Event
18 June 1940	De Gaulle declaration	18 June 1940	Erwin, Rosalie and Gitta leave Vichy, refugees, no luggage
June 1940	German armies advancing		
20 June 1940	Bayonne and Bordeaux fall		
June 1940	Vichy France	27 June 1940	Arrive Le Perthus, Spanish frontier closed
		9 July 1940	Erwin, Rosalie and Gitta leave Le Perthus
		22 July 1940	Erwin, Rosalie and Gitta arrive in Casablanca
8 Aug–10 Oct 1940	Naval battles, Battle of Britain	14 Sept 1940	Erwin, Rosalie and Gitta leave Casablanca
		18 Sept 1940	Erwin, Rosalie and Gitta arrive in Lisbon
		19 Sept–5 Oct 1940	Erwin, Rosalie and Gitta in Lisbon prison
		8 Oct 1940	Erwin, Rosalie and Gitta arrive in Gibraltar

World events		Family events	
Date	Event	Date	Event
		25 Oct 1940	Erwin, Rosalie and Gitta arrive in Liverpool
		28 Oct 1940	Erwin, Rosalie and Gitta arrive in London
27 May 1942	Czech parachutists ambushed Heydrich's car, killed him, 2,300 Czechs executed at Lidice		
April 1944	Deportation of Hungarian Jews	April 1944	Grandparents to Auschwitz, Béla disappears
6 June 1944	Allied offensive in Europe		
8 May 1945	Victory in Europe		
6 Aug 1945	Hiroshima		
12 Sept 1945	End of World War II		
		July 1961	First trip to Budapest
		April 1962	Erwin's death
		July 1976	Rosalie's death
Oct 1989	Collapse of Berlin Wall		
		Aug 1991	First return to Bratislava
		Nov 1997	Anny's death

Map of Europe and North Africa before World War II, from Czech school atlas